Psalm 37:4

In Loving Memory of
Sylvia W. Turner
09/03/1946-06/06/2016

Sylvia's whole life was lovingly spent with and sharing the written word in various forms. A wordsmith in her own right, she transcribed and proofread professionally the medical records of literally hundreds of thousands of people over her lifetime and she so loved God, the Bible, the art of writing, poetry, and life.

Presented To:

_____

From:

_____

Date:

_____

Praise for
Desires of Your Heart, Angels & Cowboys and Life's Highway and Dusty Trails

"Michael has a gift and writes from his heart. He is a true man of God and his words have touched many lives. He sees the beauty in others and shares his life experiences, insights and feelings with honesty and love."- Nancy from Illinois

"......his poems have touched my heart.......the poems this gifted man writes are a true inspiration to us all. Michael brings our Heavenly Father's guidance and words of scripture in layman's terms." - Melody from Texas

"A good honest read from the heart. I could never relate much to the Bible until I started reading this man's books. The way he ties in scripture verses to every story seems to now make the Bible come alive for me as it never did before." - Jack from Missouri

"Your poems saved me Michael; they touched my heart and gave me Peace, the kind that surpasses all understanding. And then you would arm me with the written word and those scriptures became my armor and my shield and soon, I wasn't so sad or discouraged or even ashamed. I'm proud to be a child of God, a horse lover, a cowgirl with those old fashioned morals."- Maura from Arizona

"Desires of Your Heart will help you open your heart to hear God speak to you day by day. Your spirit will overflow, as you are embraced by the One who loves you more than you can imagine."- Debra from Kansas

"One of the most well written books I have ever read. Each story touches a part of my life in some way. A GREAT spiritual book that I think will even be a BIGGER success than it already is as the public discovers this one. Keep writing Michael Gasaway you have a WINNER on your hands." – Maddie from Georgia

"Inspiring, uplifting. Love it!" – Margaret from Iowa

"It's like he has a backseat to my life and knows what I'm feeling." – Jackie from Florida

"I love Michael Gasaway's poetry! His stories are of life and the way he turns life situations into words is so touching and truly amazing. I recommend this book to anyone who loves a good read." – Nancy from Colorado

"Your book has brought much comfort to my heart..." - Maria from Nevada

"You will not be disappointed in his heartfelt writes! A wonderful book! Buy more than one and share to bless others!" – Cherie from Iowa

"I really enjoyed reading this book of poems and the scriptures that apply to the poem. It is very inspirational and thought provoking. I highly recommend it to everyone seeking comfort and inspiration for your life." - Linda from Texas

"I really like it. Makes me leave the days problems and go away. I would like to buy more of his work." - Donna from Oklahoma

"This book is more than just any average book it will speak directly to your heart and the places that need to be filled with encouragement and hope. This book besides my Bible itself is so encouraging and full of hope. I truly know it will bless your heart and encourage you!! Truly has a gift for writing from the heart and touches the soul!! Highly recommend this book, it will bless you!! Thank you Michael for your amazing gift of encouragement and writing!!" – Tiffany from Minnesota

"Your words are a blessing. God has given you the gift of writing poems. Thank you for this.....it spoke to my heart." – Judy from California

"He just seems to reach in and touch my heart with his words." – Cindy from Oregon

"Truly a gifted writer that just seems to know what a woman is feeling and thinking. His stories really touch home with so much of my past and hopefully my future." – Irene from Oklahoma

"His books read like a good country song. They seem to touch on all aspects of life from a western (my) perspective." – Jim from Texas

Life's Highway
and
Dusty Trails

Stories of Love and Life Written in Rhyme

MICHAEL GASAWAY

Published by Diamond G Publishing.

Scriptures were taken from the King James Version of the Holy Bible. Public Domain.

Scriptures were taken from the Holy Bible, New International Version ®, NIV ®. Copyright © 1973, 1978, 1984, 2011, by Biblica, Inc. ™ Used by permission of Zondervan, All rights reserved worldwide. www.zondervan.com The "NIV" and "New International Version" are trademarks registered in the United States Patent Trademark Office by Biblica, Inc. ™ Used by permission

Scriptures taken from the New King James Version®.
Copyright © 1982 by Thomas Nelson, Used by permission.
. All rights reserved.

Scripture quotations are from the ESV® Bible (The Holy Bible, English Standard Version®), copyright © 2001 by Crossway, a publishing ministry of Good News Publishers. Used by permission. All rights reserved.

Cover painting by Denny Karchner. Contact Denny at his web site for more information on this or other western art. **www.karchnerwesternart.com**

Graphic design, front and back cover art by Denny Karchner.

The cover art work is from an oil painting by my good friend Denny Karchner and is titled Tom Mix – Hell Bent For Leather 1928. It features the famous silent-era cowboy movie star, Tom Mix. The photo of Mix that Denny used as a reference was an old black and white photo likely taken where he lived in Oklahoma. The famous Henderson motorcycle used in the paiting was manufactured in Detroit from 1912 until 1933. The classic bi-plane that Denny chose for the background is a famous 1928 Boeing Army 100/P-12 which now resides in the Museum of Flight in Seattle, WA. Denny thought it would be most appropriate to paint Mix racing through Monument Valley as a backdrop.

Back cover photograph by Carol McEver Maceikis

ISBN-13:978-0692793756 ISBN-10:0692793755

This book is dedicated to my family, friends, and anyone that has journeyed down "Life's Highway or Dusty Trail" in search of your dream. To my sons of whom I'm so proud of the men and great examples you have become. To my youngest son Sammy that now inspires us all from heaven above. "You inspire me daily Sammy and I think it's really time for me to go climb our mountain again. See you at the top!"

I hope these poems put a smile on your face, a song in your heart or maybe a tear in your eye when you remember back to that first hello or last goodbye. Remember you're never too young or too old to seek out and follow your dreams.
God Bless, Never Give Up and Keep Dreamin'.

Thank you to my many Facebook followers who have taken this journey in rhyme with me. Your comments have been very motivational and kept me writing when I was wondering if it was doing any good.

Follow me on Facebook at: **https://www.facebook.com/michaelthepoetryman** and at my website: **http://www.michaelgasaway.com/**

Thank you everyone that has offered suggestions for poems. I hope you see a story written in rhyme within these pages that bring you inspiration, hope, faith and peace.

A special thank you goes out to those very exceptional people who inspired many of these poems. May God grant you the desires of your heart and make all your dreams come true.

I would like to extend a very special thank you to Denny Karchner for his time and efforts in producing the graphic art work and cover painting for my books and to Leigh Karchner for her editing and proofing abilities.

Thank you God for guiding my pen that wrote these words. Thank you God for providing me with the inspiration that has reached so many hearts and keeps touching and changing so many lives.

Guide to Story Themes

Adversity: 18, 28, 32, 34, 36, 38, 52, 64, 66, 72, 78, 86, 88, 90, 94, 98, 100, 106, 108, 112, 116, 124, 130, 134, 136, 140, 146, 152, 154

Attitude: 10, 20, 22, 27, 32, 48, 52, 58, 68, 84, 90, 96, 112, 124, 126, 128, 130, 132, 134, 136, 140, 142, 146, 150

Believe: 8, 10, 20, 34, 48, 56, 62, 68, 84, 86, 88, 90, 96, 104, 108, 112, 116, 126, 128, 134, 136, 138, 142, 146, 148, 152, 154

Brokenness: 16, 18, 20, 30, 32, 34, 38, 48, 66, 80, 94, 98, 100, 106, 112, 130, 136, 146

Change: 10, 20, 22, 26, 32, 34, 38, 42, 48, 52, 60, 88, 96, 112, 126, 130, 136, 140, 146, 154

Choices: 8, 10, 18, 20, 22, 26, 28, 30, 32, 34, 38, 40, 42, 48, 52, 50, 54, 56, 60, 68, 70, 74, 84, 86, 88, 90, 94, 96, 100, 104, 112, 120, 124, 128, 130, 132, 134, 136, 138, 140, 142, 146, 150, 154

Closure & Fear: 20, 28, 30, 32, 34, 90, 98, 106, 112, 116, 136 146,

Desires: 8, 10, 14, 26, 42, 44, 46, 48, 50, 54, 56, 58, 60, 62, 64, 68, 76, 78, 80, 82, 108, 110, 112, 130, 132, 136, 142, 144, 146

Dreams: 10, 26, 38, 42, 44, 46, 48, 50, 56, 58, 60, 64, 68, 76, 78, 80, 82, 92, 104, 112, 114, 118, 124, 128, 132, 134, 142, 146

Destiny: 10, 16, 20, 28, 44, 48, 54, 60, 74, 84, 86, 108, 142, 154

Faith: 10, 20, 22, 24, 32, 46, 48, 56, 60, 64, 70, 74, 84, 90, 98, 106, 108, 112, 116, 124, 134, 136, 140, 142, 146, 148, 154

Happiness & Blessings: 8, 10, 16, 38, 42, 44, 50, 52, 54, 58, 60, 68, 74, 82, 88, 96, 110, 112, 120, 126, 128, 134, 140, 142, 148, 150

Holidays: 30, 36, 122, 132, 148, 152

Hope & Peace: 10, 14, 18, 24, 44, 54, 68, 72, 88, 138, 140

Loss & Pain: 18, 30, 32, 34, 36, 54, 64, 66, 72, 78, 80, 94, 98, 100, 102, 106, 136, 154

Love: 8, 10, 14, 16, 22, 24, 26, 30, 36, 40, 42, 44, 50, 56, 60, 62, 68, 80, 82, 86, 92, 104, 108, 110, 112, 114, 116, 118, 120, 130, 132, 134, 142, 144, 146, 148, 154

War/Stress/PTSD: 20, 26, 28, 30, 32, 34, 36, 54, 62, 70, 74, 78, 90, 100, 102, 128, 146

Memories: 12, 14, 16, 18, 20, 30, 38, 42, 48, 54, 66, 72, 76, 78, 80, 98, 110, 114, 120, 140, 146, 148, 150

Music: 12, 14, 16, 18, 40, 126

New Beginnings: 8, 10, 14, 16, 18, 20, 22, 32, 38, 42, 46, 56, 60, 64, 66, 72, 74, 78, 84, 92, 98, 100, 104, 110, 112, 114, 116, 118, 120, 128, 130, 132, 134, 136, 140, 142, 144, 154

Never Give Up: 16, 28, 32, 34, 46, 52, 58, 60, 62, 64, 66, 68, 70, 78, 82, 84, 86, 104, 102, 112, 108, 116, 118, 128, 130, 136, 142, 144, 146, 154

Passion: 14, 16, 28, 50, 52, 54, 56, 58, 80, 62, 64, 68, 110, 112, 114, 116, 120, 124, 126, 142, 144

Thankfulness: 16, 64, 74, 76, 78, 88, 90, 92, 96, 100, 116, 122, 134, 136, 138, 148, 150, 152, 154

Trust: 10, 18, 20, 22, 28, 44, 68, 72, 74, 78, 86, 90, 98, 102, 108, 136, 138, 146, 154

Table of Contents in Alphabetical Order

Michael Gasaway

Life's Highway and Dusty Trails

Sometimes life's highway will take you places you've never
dreamed;
Mountains so tall, deserts so vast and vistas you've never seen.

Doors will open and doors will close as you travel down life's dusty
trail;
Some will take you to heaven on earth and others through hell.

We all reach a cross roads at times as we travel through life;
One road brings you happiness and joy and the other heartache
and strife.

You always have a choice as to which highway you'll take;
Some roads will take you in circles and others to your life's fate.

Life is full of choices and it's up to you if you win or lose;
Always pray to God so that the right one you'll always choose.

Another choice she was now facing and she prayed to God which
way to go;
Her choice was now made and through her prayers the way He did
show.

Now back in Texas and in the hill country for years the place she
had longed;
It was the one place in the world that she always felt she belonged.

The desires of her heart have been fulfilled at long last;
Her and that special cowboy now walked hand n' hand leaving what
was in their past.

~~~

8

And we know that in all things God works for the good of those who love him, who have been called according to his purpose. Romans 8:28

Trust in the LORD with all thine heart; and lean not unto thine own understanding. In all thy ways acknowledge him, and he shall direct thy paths. Proverbs 3:5-6

Therefore I say unto you, What things so ever ye desire, when ye pray, believe that ye receive them, and ye shall have them. Mark 11:24

I can do all things through Christ which strengthened me. Philippians 4:13

Delight thyself also in the LORD: and he shall give thee the desires of thine heart. Psalm 37:4

For he says, "In a favorable time I listened to you, and in a day of salvation I have helped you." Behold, now is the favorable time; behold, now is the day of salvation. 2 Corinthians 6:2

How much better to get wisdom than gold! To get understanding is to be chosen rather than silver. Proverbs 16:16

Michael Gasaway

Hopeless or Hopeful Romantic

A hopeless romantic is what she is and that is so plain to see;
But a hopeful romantic is what she strives for and prays one day to
be.

True romance and love seems to have eluded her in the past
years;
But on she goes now putting aside her uncertainties, doubts and
fears.

She knows in her heart that she must first step out on faith and
perceive;
How else can you move forward in life if you don't first really see
and then believe?

I know that trying to achieve your hopes and dreams is far easier
said than done;
They sometimes are held hostage in your heart for years as life's
race you try to run.

Liberate your emotions and feelings letting them go into the crisp
autumn breeze;
Seek out your hearts desires and the petitions of your spirit and
now set your priorities.

It's now your turn and time to really let it go and truly start living
life again;
No longer is it a matter of how any more it's now just a matter of
when.

So let this day be your new beginning and for you a fresh new
start;
This is the inauguration of your new life's voyage and it's time for
you to embark.

Say a prayer to God above and seek His guidance remembering
that it's a marathon not a sprint in life's race;
God will guide your steps always and be there at life's finish line
with His loving embrace.

~~~

Delight thyself also in the Lord: and he shall give thee the desires of thine heart. Psalm 37:4

Be careful for nothing; but in everything by prayer and supplication with thanksgiving let your requests be made known unto God. And the peace of God, which passes all understanding, shall keep your hearts and minds through Christ Jesus. Philippians 4:6-7

Now faith is the substance of things hoped for, the evidence of things not seen. Hebrews 11:1

Rejoice in hope, be patient in tribulation, be constant in prayer. Romans 12:12

If any of you lacks wisdom, let him ask God, who gives generously to all without reproach, and it will be given him. James 1:5

This is the confidence we have in approaching God: that if we ask anything according to his will, he hears us. And if we know that he hears us—whatever we ask—we know that we have what we asked of him. 1 John 5:14-15

Likewise the Spirit helps us in our weakness. For we do not know what to pray for as we ought, but the Spirit himself intercedes for us with groaning too deep for words. Romans 8:26

For God hath not given us the spirit of fear; but of power, and of love, and of a sound mind. 2 Timothy 1:7

A man's heart deviseth his way: but the Lord directeth his steps. Proverbs 16:9

The Songs

They are the singers of the songs that stand on the stage each
night;
Sometimes taking us back remembering a time and place where
everything felt so right.

Music like nothing else seems to just take us on a journey back in
time;
It brings back memories of another day as we listen to those words
in rhyme.

Putting a smile on your face or a song in your heart and maybe a
tear in your eye;
As you think back to that special time and remember that first kiss
or last goodbye.

Oh how it can reach down into your very soul and touch your
heart;
Taking you back into the past or leading you forward toward a new
start.

Country music seems to touch us deep inside like no other kind of
song;
Telling us of a happier time or maybe how that one love went so
wrong.

The songs these troubadours do sing each night up on that stage;
There they send the crowd into a frenzy of delight with a musical
rage.

We have all felt it at one time or another as we hear some ole'
song sung;
Memories come flooding back in as we recall how it all came
undone.

Yes music is a harbinger of times both good and bad we have
stored away;
Each of us has that special song that transports us back to that
special day.

So treasure those songs when you hear them played and memories
they convey;
Without us ever realizing why, sometimes it just seems to happen
that way.

Next time a special song catches your ear, remember with whom
and the time and place;
Somewhere in your tomorrows down life's highway it will come
back to you with God's special grace.

~~~

*Speaking to one another with psalms, hymns, and songs from the
Spirit. Sing and make music from your heart to the Lord,
Ephesians 5:19*

*Is any among you afflicted? let him pray. Is any merry? let him
sing psalms. James 5:13*

*I can do all things through Christ which strengthened me.
Philippians 4:13*

*Whoever sings songs to a heavy heart is like one who takes off a
garment on a cold day, and like vinegar on soda.
Proverbs 25:20*

*My heart, O God, is steadfast, my heart is steadfast;
I will sing and make music. Psalm 57:7*

*I will sing unto the LORD as long as I live: I will sing praise to my
God while I have my being. Psalm 104:33*

Michael Gasaway

Neon Lights and Old Barstools

She sat on the bench at the water's edge and played her 'ole
guitar;
At times it seemed like a life time ago and yet really not that far.

It was where she found peace with each new song she wrote;
Music was her life now and seemed to be the one thing that gave
her hope.

Neon lights and old barstools and singing those songs in rhyme;
This had been her heart's desire and was now coming true in three
quarter time.

Days on the road took their toll and were hard and lonelier still;
In her heart she still had a dream of a good man and a family to
fulfill.

The years passed by, sometimes fast other times so very slow;
Then she met that special cowboy and true love started to flow.

Now her life is complete and everything she always wanted it to
be;
She still remembers with fondness when with a yellow rose on one
knee he asked, "Will you marry me".

~~~

Now may the Lord of peace himself give you peace at all times in every way. The Lord be with you all. 2 Thessalonians 3:16

Delight yourself in the LORD, and he will give you the desires of your heart. Psalm 37:4

Love is patient and kind; love does not envy or boast; it is not arrogant or rude. It does not insist on its own way; it is not irritable or resentful; it does not rejoice at wrongdoing, but rejoices with the truth. Love bears all things, believes all things, hopes all things, endures all things. 1 Corinthians 13:4-7

And above all these put on love, which binds everything together in perfect harmony. Colossians 3:14

My heart, O God, is steadfast, my heart is steadfast; I will sing and make music. Psalm 57:7

I will sing unto the LORD as long as I live: I will sing praise to my God while I have my being. Psalm 104:33

15

Michael Gasaway

Singer in the Band

It was his first night out on the town since he couldn't remember
when;
His heart had been broken but felt now it was finally on the mend.

There she sat with midnight hair stretching down her back;
Looking at him she smiled, nothing did this cowgirl seem to lack.

With teeth as white as cotton in the fall and eyes like bluebonnets
in the spring;
Gazing it seemed into his very soul, then standing she strolled over
walking up on the stage to sing.

After a few songs she motioned for him to come up front to the
stage light;
She knelt down and whispered, Cowboy this song is just for you
tonight.

Singing a song she just had written of new love and soul mates
that God did deliver;
Staring deep into his crystal brown eyes as she sang, sending
within his soul a peaceful quiver.

After she finished the set he asked if he could buy her a drink and
talk;
"I'd rather go outside for a bit with you and just talk and walk."

She told him that was a first as she'd never done that to anyone
before;
But something inside spoke to me she said saying this is the one I
sent for you to forever adore.

The mysteries of love and life no one seems to understand;
Like how a cowboy came together that night with the singer in the
band.

The years have gone by and her music has made her a country
music star;
She still thanks God for bringing that special cowboy that night into
the bar.

Happily married for years living down on their ranch deep in the
heart of Texas;
Now she only performs on occasion and they always travel
together be it to Nashville or Vegas.

So never give up on love or finding that special lady or man in your
life;
Then one day under a Texas sky you too will become someone's
loving and devoted husband or wife.

~~~

Casting all your anxieties on him, because he cares for you.
1 Peter 5:7

There is no fear in love; but perfect love casts out fear, because
fear involves torment. But he who fears has not been made perfect
in love.1 John 4:18

Let us not become weary in doing good, for at the proper time we
will reap a harvest if we do not give up. Galatians 6:9

For I know the thoughts that I think toward you, saith the LORD,
thoughts of peace, and not of evil, to give you an expected end.
Jeremiah 29:11

Be ye strong therefore, and let not your hands be weak: for your
work shall be rewarded. 2 Chronicles 15:7

Beloved, let us love one another, for love is from God, and
whoever loves has been born of God and knows God. Anyone who
does not love does not know God, because God is love.
1 John 4:7-8

Michael Gasaway

The Music She Hears

Sitting at her piano she let her fingers dance across the keys, both black and white;
For her it had been yet another dark and sleepless lonely night.

The white keys seem to bring out a happy tune and time in her mind;
While those black keys took her back to a sad and lonely time.

Sometimes past memories and losses seem to come flooding back into her heart;
Try as she might to stop them, those memories of her past would always be a part.

In her heart she knew it was now time to let go and really move on;
Her hopes seemed to brighten with the painted sky of this new dawn.

If you allow it, grief and mourning can take on a life of its very own;
It's up to you to trust in God as with Him you'll never walk alone.

The choice is yours to move on in life or keep living in the past;
You can move forward and choose happiness and peace or keep feeling downcast.

Keep a smile on your face and a song of praise in your heart;
As with each new day, God will bring you a brand new start.

Let the past drift by like the notes of an old sad love song;
Just keep moving forward as that's where you now belong.

So let your music sooth your soul and bring you peace within;
Don't get stuck in the past as it's now time for you to begin again.

Now the music she hears and plays seems to bring her a special peace inside;
She chose to travel forward and into a bright future she does ride with God by her side.

~~~

I will sing to the LORD, because he has dealt bountifully with me.
Psalm 13:6

Is anyone among you suffering? Let him pray. Is anyone cheerful?
Let him sing praise. James 5:13

"Blessed are those who mourn, for they shall be comforted.
Matthew 5:4

And we know that for those who love God all things work together
for good, for those who are called according to his purpose.
Romans 8:28

Let us come into his presence with thanksgiving; let us make a
joyful noise to him with songs of praise! Psalm 95:2

Let the word of Christ dwell in you richly, teaching and
admonishing one another in all wisdom, singing psalms and hymns
and spiritual songs, with thankfulness in your hearts to God.
Colossians 3:16

My heart, O God, is steadfast, my heart is steadfast;
I will sing and make music. Psalm 57:7

I will sing unto the LORD as long as I live: I will sing praise to my
God while I have my being. Psalm 104:33

Delight thyself also in the LORD: and he shall give thee the desires
of thine heart. Psalm 37:4

Baggage From The Past

We all carry some with us in our travels down life's highway it
seems;
Baggage from our past that's full of heartaches and broken
dreams.

Some carry so many suitcases like they're going on an around the
world trip;
Others just an overnight bag and they carry that with a loose grip.

It should fit under the seat in front of you I always say;
And even that don't be afraid to leave it behind and just walk
away.

Maybe just a few recollections that you carry in your saddlebags
along the dusty trail;
Many memories are so entwined and aren't that easy to separate
or really curtail.

You can never actually move on if you still carry all that distressing
baggage about;
If you do then you'll always find yourself in the middle of an
emotional drought.

Perhaps you'll find that one special person that is willing and able
to help you truly unpack;
Allow them to assist you sorting it out and then really let it all go
and never look back.

Start a new life leaving all the distress, regrets and uncertainties
far behind;
Then let your mind, heart and soul once again become aligned.

Your future will be so much brighter with less stress you'll have to
bare;
Put your faith in God and then move forward into tomorrow without
a care.

God will always be there to lead guide and direct your steps along
the way;
Just let it go and to Him reach out daily in prayer asking for his
guidance and you'll never go astray.

~~~

Casting all your care upon him; for he cares for you.
1 Peter 5:7

Therefore, since we are surrounded by so great a cloud of witnesses, let us also lay aside every weight, and sin which clings so closely, and let us run with endurance the race that is set before us, Hebrews 12:1

Brothers and sisters, I do not consider myself yet to have taken hold of it. But one thing I do: Forgetting what is behind and straining toward what is ahead, Philippians 3:13

And we know that all things work together for good to them that love God, to them who are the called according to his purpose. Romans 8:28

I press toward the mark for the prize of the high calling of God in Christ Jesus. Philippians 3:14

Remember ye not the former things, neither consider the things of old. Behold, I will do a new thing; now it shall spring forth; shall ye not know it? I will even make a way in the wilderness, and rivers in the desert. Isaiah 43:18-19

Trust in the Lord with all thine heart; and lean not unto thine own understanding. In all thy ways acknowledge him, and he shall direct thy paths. Proverbs 3:5-6

And ye shall know the truth, and the truth shall make you free. John 8:32

For I know the plans I have for you, declares the Lord, plans for welfare and not for evil, to give you a future and a hope. Jeremiah 29:11

Pillars of Love

You both must be **spiritually** connected with God and each other
to be completely in love;
Both of you must first have a close and personal relationship with
God above.

Emotionally you both must be in tune so that you can help each
other through;
As there will be times when one or the other is down and feeling
blue.

Together **intellectually** you have to be connected in much the
same way;
For if not your minds may be too different and your love becoming
passé.

In all ways you must be open **communicatively** about everything
that touches your lives;
You must communicate not only in words but spiritually,
emotionally, intellectually and physically to decide.

Physically you have to be connected as this is what truly binds
you together as one;
This however must be the last pillar or everything else in time may
come undone.

Too many people rush into a relationship out of order putting
physical first in line;
Though this is important without the others in step you will likely
drift apart in time.

The pillars of love are what make a relationship stand the test of
time and stress;
You both must be aligned in all ways to pass many of life's tests.

So next time you enter a relationship remember the steps and with
God take them one by one;
Then your love will be complete and grow stronger by day and
never come undone.

~~~

For we wrestle not against flesh and blood, but against principalities, against powers, against the rulers of the darkness of this world, against spiritual wickedness in high places. Ephesians 6:12

Then Peter said unto them, Repent, and be baptized every one of you in the name of Jesus Christ for the remission of sins, and ye shall receive the gift of the Holy Ghost. Acts 2:38 KJV

Likewise, husbands, live with your wives in an understanding way, showing honor to the woman….. 1 Peter 3:7

Therefore confess your sins to each other and pray for each other so that you may be healed. The prayer of a righteous person is powerful and effective. James 5:16

Behold, I stand at the door and knock. If anyone hears My voice and opens the door, I will come in to him and dine with him, and he with Me. Revelation 3:20

So then faith cometh by hearing, and hearing by the word of God. Romans 10:17

The Song of Songs, which is Solomon's. Let him kiss me with the kisses of his mouth! For your love is better than wine; Song of Solomon 1:1-2

Love is patient, love is kind. It does not envy, it does not boast, it is not proud. It does not dishonor others, it is not self-seeking, it is not easily angered, it keeps no record of wrongs. Love does not delight in evil but rejoices with the truth. It always protects, always trusts, always hopes, always perseveres. Love never fails. 1 Corinthians 13:4-8

Michael Gasaway

Drop of Rain

One day when I was feeling down and out;
I asked God to explain love to me so that about it I'd have no
doubt.

He said that I will put it in a way that you can understand and see;
Just how much I love you my child and with you I will always be.

Picture a drop of rain as equal to one part of my love;
This I freely send to you from heaven here above.

Look at the ocean stretching out before you far and wide;
Observe all the drops of rain (love) that made it and you can see
the love inside.

See one drop of rain as true unconditional love from me;
Now you can see how vast my love for you is and truly believe.

If one drop of rain is equal to one part of my love from above;
You can understand just how deep for you and vast is my love.

The next time an ocean, lake or rain storm you happen to see;
Just remember how much I love you and with you I will always be.

~~~

For God so loved the world, that he gave his only begotten Son, that whosoever believeth in him should not perish, but have everlasting life. John 3:16

But God commendeth his love toward us, in that, while we were yet sinners, Christ died for us. Romans 5:8

There is no fear in love; but perfect love casteth out fear: because fear hath torment. He that feareth is not made perfect in love. 1 John 4:18

In this the love of God was made manifest among us, that God sent his only Son into the world, so that we might live through him. In this is love, not that we have loved God but that he loved us and sent his Son to be the propitiation for our sins. Beloved, if God so loved us, we also ought to love one another. No one has ever seen God; if we love one another, God abides in us and his love is perfected in us. 1 John 4:9-12

And we have known and believed the love that God hath to us. God is love; and he that dwelleth in love dwelleth in God, and God in him. 1 John 4:16

Michael Gasaway

Graduation Day

I see him standing there erect and stoic before the crowd;
Once he was a boy, now a man stood before me so proud.

He had that look in his eye I had seen in my past;
That look of determination and pride to have finished this task.

His bearing, stature and look all seemed to have changed this boy I
knew;
Now here he stands a man proudly in his dress blues.

The flags flutter in the breeze and I hear the band play the songs;
And I know in my heart to this new world he now belongs.

This is not a world of childish games and idle play;
It is a deadly serious world he now enters on this his graduation
day.

I know that never the same will he ever be;
But a pride for him seems to just overwhelm me.

Today he has finished one test along life's road;
The lessons learned here will follow him where ever he goes.

There he stands on this sacred ground where so many stood
before;
He is now a proud member of the Corps.

He can now claim that title that so many strive but few ever see;
Yes, now he can say; I am a United States Marine!

~~~

For I know the plans I have for you, declares the Lord, plans for welfare and not for evil, to give you a future and a hope.
Jeremiah 29:11

Trust in the Lord with all thine heart; and lean not unto thine own understanding. In all thy ways acknowledge him, and he shall direct thy paths. Proverbs 3:5-6

So then, just as you received Christ Jesus as Lord, continue to live your lives in him, rooted and built up in him, strengthened in the faith as you were taught, and overflowing with thankfulness.
Colossians 2:6-7

When you pass through the waters, I will be with you; And through the rivers, they shall not overflow you. When you walk through the fire, you shall not be burned,
Nor shall the flame scorch you. Isaiah 43:2

Have not I commanded thee? Be strong and of a good courage; be not afraid, neither be thou dismayed: for the LORD thy God is with thee whithersoever thou goest. Joshua 1:9

Blessed be the LORD my Rock, Who trains my hands for war, And my fingers for battle—Psalm 144:1

Michael Gasaway

Green Ghost

Like misty vapors out of the jungle they came;
They are dressed in camo with faces painted green.

Moving swift and silent across the ground;
By the enemy they were not to be found.

Each man carried his load to bear;
Into their eyes you could see that thousand yard stare.

Green ghost they came to be known across the land;
Always at deaths door they would make their stand.

Swift, silent and deadly was their motto as is now;
Brother warriors together always on the prowl.

From the sky above or the sea below;
Where they'll come from, you will not know.

These warriors that move silent and unseen;
Proud men are they, known as Recon Marines.

With gold wings upon their chest;
These are silent warriors of our nation's best.

They live by a warrior's creed;
"Always beside you" is where they will always be.

So lift up a toast to these brave men of valor;
They will face every test and never will they cower.

~~~

A time to love, and a time to hate; a time of war, and a time of peace. Ecclesiastes 3:8

And the angel of the L<small>ORD</small> appeared unto him, and said unto him, "The L<small>ORD</small> is with thee, thou mighty man of valor." Judges 6:12

Blessed be the L<small>ORD</small> my Rock, Who trains my hands for war, And my fingers for battle—Psalm 144:1

Yea, though I walk through the valley of the shadow of death, I will fear no evil: for thou art with me; thy rod and thy staff they comfort me. Psalms 23:4

When you go to war against your enemies and see horses and chariots and an army greater than yours, do not be afraid of them, because the L<small>ORD</small> your God, who brought you up out of Egypt, will be with you. Deuteronomy 20:1

Thou art my battle axe and weapons of war: for with thee will I break in pieces the nations, and with thee will I destroy kingdoms; Jeremiah 51:20

Be on your guard; stand firm in the faith; be courageous; be strong. 1 Corinthians 16:13

Michael Gasaway

Lest We Forget

In silent rows of marble stone;
Each tells the story of our nation's own.

Long rows as far as you can see;
Pay tribute to those who died for Liberty.

Each marks the grave in silent prayer;
Of a warrior that is buried there.

They gave full measure and paid the price;
All made the ultimate sacrifice.

Today and every day do bow your head;
Pray for each of our honored dead.

Lest we forget to see;
That if not for them, many today would not be free.

Thank God for those that did give their all;
When each time that our nation did call.

I salute you and say a prayer;
As many a brother warrior I have buried there.

May God Bless and Semper Fi, with fair winds and following seas;
Until once again beside you, I will forever be.

~~~

Greater love hath no man than this, that a man lay down his life for his friends. John 15:13

Let him turn away from evil and do good; Let him seek peace and pursue it. 1 Peter 3:11

I thank God whom I serve, as did my ancestors, with a clear conscience, as I remember you constantly in my prayers night and day. 2 Timothy 1:3

But as it is written, Eye hath not seen, nor ear heard, neither have entered into the heart of man, the things which God hath prepared for them that love him.1 Corinthians 2:9

that if you confess with your mouth the Lord Jesus and believe in your heart that God has raised Him from the dead, you will be saved. Romans 10:9

Peace I leave with you, my peace I give unto you: not as the world giveth, give I unto you. Let not your heart be troubled, neither let it be afraid. John 14:27

Michael Gasaway

Lost Your Way

1608 is what the bottle read, just another empty bottle by his bed;
Another sleepless night with memories and heart ache reeling
inside his head.

The years went by and another bottle helped get him past each
day;
Sometimes it seemed so hopeless, as he'd even forgot how to
pray.

It started out with just a shot or two to get him through the night;
Then before long it was an entire bottle to make it 'til daylight.

Deeper into the abyss of loneliness and despair he slowly sank;
Instead of seeking help, he just sat alone each night and drank.

First the war then the many losses that he had faced along the
way;
No one seemed to understand, the words he tried to convey.

The doctors used acronyms and fancy words they had to say;
He just became one more of the lost, along life's lonely highway.

Now at last help seemed to arrive and truly understand his past;
She showed him new ways to cope and really live at last.

No more bottles by the bed or bad dreams or wanting to be dead;
He now has a new beginning, a new hope and says prayers
instead.

If this sounds familiar and you too feel lost and have strayed;
You're not alone as many people and organizations are ready to
help you today.

Www.22Kill.com
Www.honorcouragecommitment.org
Www.vetsandplayers.org
Www.operationrockthetroops.org
Www.veteranscrisisline.net
Www.mentalhealth.va.gov
Www.battle-buddy.info

∾∾∾

Let us therefore come boldly unto the throne of grace, that we may obtain mercy, and find grace to help in time of need.
Hebrews 4:16

And ye shall know the truth, and the truth shall make you free.
John 8:32

Be anxious for nothing, but in everything by prayer and supplication, with thanksgiving, let your requests be made known to God; Philippians 4:6

I called upon the Lord in distress: the Lord answered me, and set me in a large place. The Lord is on my side; I will not fear: what can man do unto me? Psalm 118:5-6

What shall we then say to these things? If God be for us, who can be against us? Romans 8:31

Anxiety in a man's heart weighs him down, but a good word makes him glad. Proverbs 12:25

Behold, I will do a new thing; now it shall spring forth; shall ye not know it? I will even make a way in the wilderness, and rivers in the desert. Isaiah 43:19

Casting all your anxieties on him, because he cares for you.
1 Peter 5:7

So do not fear, for I am with you; do not be dismayed, for I am your God. I will strengthen you and help you; I will uphold you with my righteous right hand. Isaiah 41:10

Another Day

Another day will soon end with the setting of the summer's bright
sun;
Then the dark night begins and another battle to be won.

The nights are always the hardest when the darkness descends to
envelop me;
Sometimes I go to sleep wishing that another sunrise I'll never see.

Having been up and down on this journey as each day I try to
travel on;
Hoping and praying that a new beginning I'll see and feel with each
new dawn.

I hope like that poem I read one day I'll awake with a real smile on
my face;
And that somehow my heart will be filled with a song of His
amazing grace.

At times I feel so depressed and seem to have forgotten just how
to win;
Then I'm reminded that at times like these to just turn it all over to
him.

He is always with me and will guide me with each step that I take;
Really it's my decision to ask for guidance from Him to guide the
choices I make.

Each day brings forth a new beginning for each person to choose;
It's your choice and you get to decide if today you'll be in it to win
or feel sorry and lose.

So decide today and let God lead you to victory that He has
planned for your life;
Don't keep carrying the trials and tribulations of the past with you
causing more strife.

Step boldly into tomorrow as that's where you truly belong;
Your choice, if your heart sings a happy tune or a dirge of a sad
song.

Just never give up on your dreams and keep pressing on each and
every day;
When it seems too much to bear just turn it over to God and pray.

One day your future will be as bright as the summer's noon day
sun;
That's when you'll realize that your new future has already begun.

Thank God for this new life standing in front of you, that you now
perceive;
All it takes is trust in Him and allow God to take the lead and for
you to truly believe.

~~~

Cast all your anxiety on him because he cares for you.
1 Peter 5:7

*And let us not grow weary of doing good, for in due season we will
reap, if we do not give up. Galatians 6:9*

*Fear thou not; for I am with thee: be not dismayed; for I am thy
God: I will strengthen thee; yea, I will help thee; yea, I will uphold
thee with the right hand of my righteousness. Isaiah 41:10*

I can do all things through Christ which strengthened me.
Philippians 4:13

*And we know that all things work together for good to them that
love God, to them who are the called according to his purpose.
Romans 8:28*

For I know the plans I have for you, declares the Lord*, plans for
welfare and not for evil, to give you a future and a hope.
Jeremiah 29:11*

*For God gave us a spirit not of fear but of power and love and self-
control. 2 Timothy 1:7*

Michael Gasaway

Memorial Day

They died so that we might live free;
Of themselves they gave all as the ultimate price for Liberty.

In every clime and place they have fought and died for freedoms
sake;
And for each a Mothers' heart did break.

Some were fathers, some were brothers and all were sons;
Each gave all and a nations freedom they won.

Remember why they died today and each day hence;
Their sacrifice is wars final consequence.

Let us never forget to pay them the respect for all they gave;
Because of them, this truly is the home of the brave.

So bow your head and do pray;
For these brave men and women we honor on this, Memorial Day.

∾∾∾

Greater love has no one than this that he lay down his life for his friends. John 15:13

Peace I leave with you; my peace I give to you. Not as the world gives do I give to you. Let not your hearts be troubled, neither let them be afraid John 14:27

He makes wars cease to the end of the earth; he breaks the bow and shatters the spear; he burns the chariots with fire. Psalm 46:9

But as it is written, Eye hath not seen, nor ear heard, neither have entered into the heart of man, the things which God hath prepared for them that love him. 1 Corinthians 2:9

that if you confess with your mouth the Lord Jesus and believe in your heart that God has raised Him from the dead, you will be saved. Romans 10:9

Michael Gasaway

Back to God

There she sits by the lake and sees it vividly in her mind;
Another memory flashes by and takes her back in time.

What is her life really she thinks but a series of bad choices and
mistakes;
This was not the life she had planned and dreamed of, with so
many heart aches.

She didn't believe her dreams were all that outrageous or that hard
to attain;
Just wanted a good Christian man to love her everyday and not
cause her any pain.

That special man she could give her love, a trusted gentleman
whom she could adore;
It always seemed she made the wrong choices when it came to
opening love's door.

Hard as she tried not to let in the bitterness and mistrust it seemed
to creep into her mind;
Back to God and going to church she decided to try again this time.

Somewhere along the way she had turned away from going to
church and God above;
It was a slow process but all things worthwhile are, especially when
it comes to true love.

Now she understands that true happiness lies within her own heart
and not in some man;
Closer she has been drawn to God and reading His word and now
seems to truly understand.

Drawing closer to God so that through Him her true love must go
to find her heart;
Smiling she thinks why hadn't she done this from the very start.

Too many people make the same mistakes as they journey down
life's highway;
They rush ahead leaving God behind and wondering why later
when they have lost their way.

Get closer to God and always let Him guide your steps from heaven
above;
Then you won't find yourself in the wasteland of despair looking in
all the wrong places for love.

~~~

*Where there is no guidance, a people falls, but in an abundance of
counselors there is safety. Proverbs 11:14*

*If any of you lacks wisdom, let him ask of God, who gives to all
liberally and without reproach, and it will be given to him.
James 1:5*

*For I know the plans I have for you," declares the LORD, "plans to
prosper you and not to harm you, plans to give you hope and a
future. Jeremiah 29:11*

*Therefore I say to you, whatever things you ask when you pray,
believe that you receive them, and you will have them.
Mark 11:24*

*Love is patient and kind; love does not envy or boast; it is not
arrogant or rude. It does not insist on its own way; it is not
irritable or resentful; it does not rejoice at wrongdoing, but rejoices
with the truth. Love bears all things, believes all things, hopes all
things, endures all things. Love never ends. 1 Corinthians 13:4-7*

*Trust in the Lord with all thine heart; and lean not unto thine own
understanding. In all thy ways acknowledge him, and he shall
direct thy paths. Proverbs 3:5-6*

*And be not conformed to this world: but be ye transformed by the
renewing of your mind, that ye may prove what is that good, and
acceptable, and perfect, will of God. Romans 12:2*

Michael Gasaway

Hallelujah

The chords came sweetly from her finger tips;
Heavenly words just seemed to flow from her crimson lips.

Singing Hallelujah touching hearts from deep within her soul;
This special song seemed to bless everyone at each and every
show.

Words she sang seemed to take you back to another time;
It told of a long ago poet who spoke to God with verses in rhyme.

Lessons come from books and songs to teach us the right way;
Don't let the burdens of life allow your feet to become stuck in the
clay.

Let your life become an example for others to follow in time;
Help show others the way and how to make that final climb.

Lift up your voices and sing Hallelujah to God up above;
Let Him fill your heart with true joy, peace and love.

~~~

Speaking to yourselves in psalms and hymns and spiritual songs, singing and making melody in your heart to the Lord; Ephesians 5:19

But I have trusted in thy mercy; my heart shall rejoice in thy salvation. Psalm 13:5

Then I heard what seemed to be the voice of a great multitude, like the roar of many waters and like the sound of mighty peals of thunder, crying out, "Hallelujah! For the Lord our God the Almighty reigns. Revelation 19:6

Oh come, let us sing to the LORD; let us make a joyful noise to the rock of our salvation! Psalm 95:1

I will sing a new song unto thee, O God: upon a psaltery and an instrument of ten strings will I sing praises unto thee. Psalm 144:9

Michael Gasaway

Maybe Somewhere In Texas

Maybe up in the pan handle of Texas in Amarillo I can be found;
At the Big Texan having a thick steak and just chowing down.

Maybe down to Lubbock where those stars are always so bright;
Yes another memory of a romantic and long special Lubbock night.

Maybe the Llano Estacado just because it's there to see;
I'm sure even in that vastness there I'll also find another memory.

Maybe way down to Alpine and Marfa just to see those lights in the
sky;
Then on to Terlingua for some chili and to just ask why?

Maybe over to Bandera and I'll see that special cowgirl I once
knew;
We'll two step the night away under a Texas moon so blue.

Maybe over to San Antonio along the River Walk I'll take my
memories out for a stroll;
There're too many memories to count but my favorite is the one at
the Alamo.

Maybe down past the King Ranch across the bridge to South Padre;
There at Amberjacks I'll have a drink or two and watch the sunset
on the Laguna Madre.

Maybe you'll find me fly fishing along the flats of Matagorda Bay;
With each cast I'll be reliving the memories along the way.

Maybe over to Houston I'll go and take in the Livestock show and
rodeo;
So many times I've been there over the years just to see that big
show.

Maybe up to Nacogdoches where the piney woods are always so
green;
Oh how I remember back to that special moment and beautiful
scene.

Maybe under the bright lights of Dallas is where I can be found;
Remembering those romantic weekends we spent downtown.

Maybe to Ft. Worth and ole Cow Town and have a beer and dinner at H3 I'll go;
Then across the street to Mavericks and get decked out from head to toe.

Maybe at College Station on a Saturday just to watch the Aggies play, you'll find me;
I won't stay long as another memory waits for me over in the Hill Country.

Maybe down around Austin on 6th street is where I'll stay;
Memories of a George Strait concert and meeting him back stage.

Maybe down to Gruene and dinner at The Gristmill under the stars overlooking the Guadalupe;
Then to Gruene Hall and dance the night away to a red dirt Band on that famous stage.

Maybe I'll go over to Fredericksburg and I'll go out and climb Enchanted Rock;
Carrying my memories of Sammy with me as I climb to the top and remembering the Hawk.

Maybe over near Concan along The Frio River is where I'll be found;
Just my Texas Angel and I is where I'll finally settle down.

~~~

And you shall write on them all the words of this law, when you cross over to enter the land that the LORD your God is giving you, a land flowing with milk and honey, as the LORD, the God of your fathers, has promised you. Deuteronomy 27:3

And I will give to you and to your offspring after you the land of your sojourning...........Genesis 17:8

By faith he went to live in the land of promise,......... Hebrews 11:9

For when I have brought them into the land flowing with milk and honey,.......Deuteronomy 31:20

Spring Time in Texas

The winds of fate seemed to drive him on as the further south he
drove;
It was just another hour or so and he'd be back in San Antonio.

It was spring time in Texas and the bluebonnets were all around;
In his heart he hoped that this time with her, maybe true love
could be found.

They were to meet in the lobby of the La Mansion Hotel along the
river walk that day.
Her beauty was beyond compare, sky blue eyes and with hair like
summer hay.

With the tip of his hat, a "Hello Darlin' and a kiss upon her hand;
Both were treasuring this special moment and feeling so grand.

Hand n' hand along the river walk that night they did stroll;
They spoke of life and love and of a future yet to unfold.

Sometimes in love and life you just have to trust God above;
Put your trust in Him and let go, as He leads you to your perfect
love.

Yes it must have been God's love all those many years ago;
Now they walk along the river with their own little boy and girl in
tow.

~~~

For I know the plans I have for you," declares the LORD, "plans to prosper you and not to harm you, plans to give you hope and a future. Jeremiah 29:11

And we know that all things work together for good to them that love God, to them who are the called according to his purpose. Romans 8:28

But above all these things put on love, which is the bond of perfection. Colossians 3:14

Now the God of hope fill you with all joy and peace in believing, that ye may abound in hope, Romans 15:13

And we have known and believed the love that God hath to us. God is love; and he that dwelleth in love dwelleth in God, and God in him. 1 John 4:16

Take delight in the LORD, and he will give you the desires of your heart. Psalm 37:4

Michael Gasaway

This Trail We Call The Ride

It was time to move on as spring was in the air;
He remembered back and knew that sometimes life wasn't fair.

But you can't give up on life or just quit and give in;
You have to cowboy up and ride on 'til the very end.

You have to sit tall in the saddle with your head held high;
Today is a new day for you along this trail we call the ride.

Sometimes the ride is difficult and at times really hard on a soul;
Just keep trusting in God and He'll always show you the way to go.

Now he was back in Texas the one place he dearly loved to be;
This was his home and vowed from here never again to leave.

Things started changing for the better, almost the day that he
arrived;
He went from just surviving to really start living and feeling alive.

His new livelihood was really taking off as God blessed him from
above;
Not only a new career and outlook had he found but also his one
true love.

So never give up and keep praying for your heart's desire and
secret dreams;
You never know when they'll arrive as they may be closer than
they seem.

~~~

And we know that all things work together for good to them that love God, to them who are the called according to his purpose. Romans 8:28

And let us not grow weary of doing good, for in due season we will reap, if we do not give up. Galatians 6:9

Trust in the LORD with all thine heart; and lean not unto thine own understanding. Proverbs 3:5

I can do all things through Christ which strengthened me. Philippians 4:13

Before I was afflicted I went astray, But now I keep Your word. Psalm 119:67

Delight thyself also in the LORD: and he shall give thee the desires of thine heart. Psalm 37:4

For the vision is yet for an appointed time, but at the end it shall speak, and not lie: though it tarry, wait for it; because it will surely come, it will not tarry. Habakkuk 2:3

Michael Gasaway

Memories or Dreams

When you cross over that river will your heart be full of memories
or dreams;
Did you live your life to the fullest pushing the edge of the seams.

Will you think back fondly on all the memories you shared;
Or did you live in fear allowing your dreams to become ensnared.

Too many people come to the end full of dreams they wished
they'd done;
So die with only memories, chasing that last dream on the run.

Life's so very short when you take time to reflect back on it all;
Too many never had the chance and were left with just their
names on a wall.

Live each day to its fullest without any pause or regret;
Climb a mountain, write a book or take your true love and dance in
the rain and get wet.

It's up to you to fulfill the dreams God gave you deep inside;
Now climb back in the saddle and ride cowboy ride.

Ride into the future chasing every dream that you can chase;
God will lead guide and direct you to the end of life's race.

Then when your final day does come and God calls you home;
A smile will cross your face as you'll be ready for heavenly pastures
to roam.

~~~

But Mary kept all these things, and pondered them in her heart. Luke 2:19

For God hath not given us the spirit of fear; but of power, and of love, and of a sound mind. 2 Timothy 1:7

Trust in the Lord with all thine heart; and lean not unto thine own understanding. In all thy ways acknowledge him, and he shall direct thy paths. Proverbs 3:5-6

For so is the will of God, that with well doing ye may put to silence the ignorance of foolish men: 1 Peter 2:15

Wherefore be ye not unwise, but understanding what the will of the Lord is. Ephesians 5:17

But, as it is written, "What no eye has seen, nor ear heard, nor the heart of man imagined, what God has prepared for those who love him"— 1 Corinthians 2:9

Delight thyself also in the Lord: and he shall give thee the desires of thine heart. Psalm 37:4

Michael Gasaway

Remember the Alamo

Her eyes were as blue as a Texas sky as seen from the hills down
Austin way;
Midnight was her hair as the night sky down along Matagorda Bay.

Sparkling were her eyes like a West Texas star filled night;
White were her teeth like cotton in the fall and just as bright.

When she spoke she sounded smooth as honey with kisses just as
sweet;
The touch of her lips upon his skin made him thank God they did
meet.

Their romance went as fast as a twister up on the pan handle
plains;
A flame of passion was ignited and could not be quenched even by
a North Texas spring rain.

Then one evening with a ring and a yellow rose in front of The
Alamo;
Down on bended knee on that spring night to her he did propose.

Almost one year to the day along the River Walk down in San
Antonio they became as one;
The years have since gone by and their love still burns as bright as
that Texas summer sun.

They have between them a love as big as Texas and just as grand;
Just as years ago when on that spot for love of Texas others had
made a stand.

Just like the battle cry that was heard so many years ago in the
past;
"Remember the Alamo" is their personal cry for a love that will
forever last.

~~~

50

Love is patient and kind; love does not envy or boast; it is not arrogant 5 or rude. It does not insist on its own way; it is not irritable or resentful; it does not rejoice at wrongdoing, but rejoices with the truth. Love bears all things, believes all things, hopes all things, endures all things. Love never ends. 1 Corinthians 13:4-8

Pleasant words are as an honeycomb, sweet to the soul, and health to the bones. Proverbs 16:24

Let him kiss me with the kisses of his mouth: for thy love is better than wine. Song of Solomon 1:2

Beloved, let us love one another: for love is of God; and every one that loveth is born of God, and knoweth God. 1 John 4:7

May he grant you your heart's desire and fulfill all your plans! Psalm 20:4

For I know the plans I have for you," declares the LORD, "plans to prosper you and not to harm you, plans to give you hope and a future. Jeremiah 29:11

And we know that all things work together for good to them that love God, to them who are the called according to his purpose. Romans 8:28

Michael Gasaway

The Last Cowboy

Riding the fence line was not the best of jobs on the ranch he
knew;
But being a cowboy was better than anything else he cared to do.

He'd been a cowboy nearly fifty years and the stories he could tell;
At times it felt like pure heaven, and then there were those times
he rode through hell.

Many a good horse he'd ridden over the years never letting him
down;
Wished he could say the same about folks, especially those that
lived in town.

Remembering back to the wild times and how it use to be;
How in his younger years he'd even survived a stampede.

Indians and outlaws all had tested him more than a time or two;
But his courage always held fast and his aim was always true.

Still he finds answers and guidance from the Good Book he reads;
Its cover is well worn like his saddle but with hope it feeds.

Starting each day with a reading and watching the sun come up;
That's how his day begins with the Bible and coffee in a tin cup.

Sometimes he wonders how much longer he can keep fighting the
strife;
He vows to keep fighting on, even if he's the last cowboy in this ole
life.

~~~

Let all that you do be done in love. 1 Corinthians 16:14

And whatsoever ye do, do it heartily, as to the Lord, and not unto men; Colossians 3:23

and to make it your ambition to lead a quiet life: You should mind your own business and work with your hands, just as we told you, so that your daily life may win the respect of outsiders and so that you will not be dependent on anybody. 1 Thessalonians 4:11-12

For the word of God is living and active, sharper than any two-edged sword, piercing to the division of soul and of spirit, of joints and of marrow, and discerning the thoughts and intentions of the heart. Hebrews 4:12

All scripture is given by inspiration of God, and is profitable for doctrine, for reproof, for correction, for instruction in righteousness: That the man of God may be perfect, thoroughly furnished unto all good works. 2 Timothy 3:16-17

Blessed is the man who remains steadfast under trial, for when he has stood the test he will receive the crown of life, which God has promised to those who love him. James 1:12

His Cowboy Life

His best days were behind him he thought as he gazed at the stars
on high;
Memories took him back to another place and time as embers
danced into the sky.

The war had changed the boy he had been into a man he didn't
recognize or know;
He had become hardened and saddened by the times, with wounds
inside that did not show.

Now with the war over he had to make a living and learn to begin
again;
But all he had learned was how to kill and every other kind of sin.

With his Colt 44 and knife he had become proficient with both;
Into this new world he returned, where there didn't seem to be any
good uses for them or any hope.

Sometimes his dreams took him back to the many battles he had
seen during the war;
Even loud sounds seemed to affect him now as they never had
before.

A soldier, buffalo hunter, lawman and cowboy he had all done in
his life;
With just his horse, rope, gun and knife, he had learned to stand
up and face any strife.

Now the years of hard livin' on the trail we're catching up with him
more each day;
Sometimes he wondered just how much longer he could continue
with his cowboy way.

It was the one life he had known for so long and the one he really
loved;
So each night he prayed that his cowboy life he could continue 'til
he was called home above.

So into the fires embers he stares and feels the night chill come
upon him way down deep;
Resting his head on his saddle, closing his eyes and off he drifts to
a cowboy's lasting and final sleep.

~~~

The glory of young men is their strength, but the splendor of old men is their gray hair. Proverbs 20:29

So we do not lose heart. Though our outer self is wasting away, our inner self is being renewed day by day. 2 Corinthians 4:16

Gray hair is a crown of glory; it is gained in a righteous life. Proverbs 16:31

Even to your old age I am he, and to gray hairs I will carry you. I have made, and I will bear; I will carry and will save. Isaiah 46:4

Blessed is the man who remains steadfast under trial, for when he has stood the test he will receive the crown of life, which God has promised to those who love him. James 1:12

Cast me not off in the time of old age; forsake me not when my strength faileth. Psalm 71:9

"For God so loved the world, that he gave his only Son, that whoever believes in him should not perish but have eternal life. John 3:16

And the dust returns to the earth as it was, and the spirit returns to God who gave it. Ecclesiastes 12:7

A time to be born, and a time to die; a time to plant, and a time to pluck up what is planted; Ecclesiastes 3:2

He will wipe away every tear from their eyes, and death shall be no more, neither shall there be mourning, nor crying, nor pain anymore, for the former things have passed away." Revelation 21:4

Michael Gasaway

Three Turns and Burn

Three turns and burn is how she came riding into his heart;
Her blonde hair was flying beneath her Stetson from the start.

Bright blue eyes sparkling and dancing in the arena lights;
Something told him this was not going to be just another rodeo
night.

There she stood as he entered the dancehall later that evening;
She stood 5'6 and looked as beautiful as the Texas spring.

Their eyes met from across the room as she strolled over to him;
Take me for a twirl on the dance floor cowboy, as she pushed back
her hat brim.

Two stepping and waltzing the night away in each other's arms;
Dance after dance they were both becoming entranced with each
other's charms.

Now they make the circuit each year always traveling side by side;
She runs the barrels and he goes for another eight second ride.

The years have passed by and they settled on a ranch down Texas
way;
Each has their own gold buckles on display.

They each had the same dream and saw it fulfilled those many
years ago;
Falling in love with that special person and ride in 'Vegas at the
Championship Rodeo.

~~~

And whatsoever ye do, do it heartily, as to the Lord, and not unto men; Colossians 3:23

Now finish the work, so that your eager willingness to do it may be matched by your completion of it, according to your means. 2 Corinthians 8:11

For I know the plans I have for you," declares the LORD, "plans to prosper you and not to harm you, plans to give you hope and a future. Jeremiah 29:11

Beloved, let us love one another: for love is of God; and every one that loveth is born of God, and knoweth God. 1 John 4:7

A slack hand causes poverty, but the hand of the diligent makes rich. Proverbs 10:4

And over all these virtues put on love, which binds them all together in perfect unity. Colossians 3:14

May he grant you your heart's desire and fulfill all your plans! Psalm 20:4

Michael Gasaway

Barrel Racer

One look in her eyes and she knew this chestnut mare was going
to be just right;
Each evening they practiced running those barrels night after
night.

Faster and faster they seemed to go, increasing their speed always
becoming more aligned;
In her heart she was sure that she was the one and this was going
to be her time.

They ran the circuit racking up points in town after town;
They were the ones to beat, and she had her sights on the crown.

Vegas was now but a few more stops down the highway;
She knew it was theirs to win or lose on that fateful day.

Those Vegas nights were so bright as in her 'ole pickup and trailer
she drove in;
It wouldn't be long and it would be their time, time for gold to win.

It seems the times just got better with each rider that before her
rode;
Now she was up and down the alley they ran in search of gold.

As they crossed the line the noise of the crowd rose in her ears;
Louder and louder it got as she knew then, it had been worth all
the hard work and tears.

~~~

And whatsoever ye do in word or deed, do all in the name of the Lord Jesus, giving thanks to God and the Father by him.
Colossians 3:17

Now finish the work, so that your eager willingness to do it may be matched by your completion of it, according to your means.
2 Corinthians 8:11

Commit your work to the LORD, and your plans will be established.
Proverbs 16:3

And whatsoever ye do, do it heartily, as to the Lord, and not unto men; Colossians 3:23

I can do all things through Christ which strengthened me.
Philippians 4:13

Everyone who competes in the games goes into strict training. They do it to get a crown that will not last, but we do it to get a crown that will last forever. 1 Corinthians 9:25

The Shamrock Ranch

Midnight hair and sparkling eyes with a manner so care free;
A spunky Irish lass was she, off on a new adventure across the
sea.

To join her father in America and help make his dreams come true;
Establishing the Black Angus breed on his ranch and see it through.

Bringing with her was a Black Angus bull with champion pedigree
within;
It was just a dream to breed him with those longhorns and a
legacy to begin.

The years have gone on and those plans did succeed in time;
Crossing the Black Angus and those Longhorns created a new
breed to find.

She took over the ranch after her father passed but kept his dream
alive;
It became one of the best beef cattle ranches in America and today
does still thrive.

Many a steer and human alike can trace their roots to this very
place;
The Shamrock Ranch still exists today and seems to be filled with
Gods amazing grace.

Yes that Irish lass fulfilled her father's dream as well as hers it
seems;
You never know where life will lead, so always follow your dreams.

~~~

Delight thyself also in the LORD*: and he shall give thee the desires of thine heart. Psalm 37:4*

Commit your work to the Lord, and your plans will be established. Proverbs 16:3

Plans fail for lack of counsel, but with many advisers they succeed. Proverbs 15:22

For I know the thoughts that I think toward you, saith the LORD*, thoughts of peace, and not of evil, to give you an expected end. Jeremiah 29:11*

For the vision is yet for an appointed time, but at the end it shall speak, and not lie: though it tarry, wait for it; because it will surely come, it will not tarry. Habakkuk 2:3

And we know that all things work together for good to them that love God, to them who are the called according to his purpose. Romans 8:28

Commit your work to the LORD*, and your plans will be established. Proverbs 16:3*

Michael Gasaway

Promise He Made

He has miles to ride yet before he can stop to sleep;
A promise he made to her that he knows he has to keep.

It's been so long ago it seems, when he rode off to that 'ole war;
Promises he made to her that he'd be back to her one day he
swore.

The bluebonnets were in bloom and reminded him of her eyes;
At night the twinkling stars reminded him of her hair like the
midnight sky.

Just a few days more riding and she'd once again be in his arms,
holding her tight.
There he'd never leave her and with her he'd be every night.

From the hill top he could see her on the porch there below;
She was wearing that yellow cotton dress he bought for her in San
Antonio.

Running up the road as she saw him ridding down the hillside;
Pulling her up in his arms, kissing away the happy tears, together
home they did ride.

The promise he made which now seems so very long in the past;
It had been those words that kept him going, finding his way back
to a true love he knew would always last.

~~~

Love is patient and kind; love does not envy or boast; it is not arrogant or rude. It does not insist on its own way; it is not irritable or resentful; it does not rejoice at wrongdoing, but rejoices with the truth. Love bears all things, believes all things, hopes all things, and endures all things. Love never ends.
1 Corinthians 13:4-9

Like a lily among thorns is my darling among the young women.
Song of Solomon 2:2

And above all these put on love, which binds everything together in perfect harmony. Colossians 3:14

So now faith, hope, and love abide, these three; but the greatest of these is love. 1 Corinthians 13:13

With all humility and gentleness, with patience, bearing with one another in love, Ephesians 4:2

Sanctify them in the truth; your word is truth. John 17:17

Michael Gasaway

Cowboy Angel

They came together on a midnight winter's eve;
The words he spoke opened up the door, making her believe.

She'd never heard such words and at times touched her heart;
Was this as she had once dreamed, her new beginning, her brand
new start?

A cowboy angel she called him as he was there when she needed
him most;
His gentle presence and words seemed to give her a new found
hope.

Some of the struggles and turmoil's she was facing had mounted
for so long;
But there he was, right beside her, keeping her safe from all
wrong.

Is he really for real she wandered at times in her mind?
With all she seems to be putting him through, how could he
continue to be so kind?

The days have passed and her healing is almost completely done;
Now she awakens each day with a smile on her face with the
dawning of the sun.

Each day she thanks God for bringing that cowboy angel into her
life;
Right beside her he stayed helping her through the pain and strife.

Sometimes God sends us human angels to help us with our
struggles and strain;
They may come when you least expect it, helping you move on
past your fears and pain.

~~~

Be not forgetful to entertain strangers: for thereby some have entertained angels unawares. Hebrews 13:2

Bless the LORD, O you his angels, you mighty ones who do his word, obeying the voice of his word! Psalm 103:20

For he shall give his angels charge over thee, to keep thee in all thy ways. Psalm 91:11

He healeth the broken in heart, and bindeth up their wounds. Psalm 147:3

The LORD is my strength and my shield; my heart trusted in him, and I am helped: therefore my heart greatly rejoiceth; and with my song will I praise him. Psalm 28:7

If I have told you earthly things, and ye believe not, how shall ye believe, if I tell you of heavenly things? John 3:12

Are not all angels ministering spirits sent to serve those who will inherit salvation? Hebrews 1:14

Fear thou not; for I am with thee: be not dismayed; for I am thy God: I will strengthen thee; yea, I will help thee; yea, I will uphold thee with the right hand of my righteousness. Isaiah 41:10

Michael Gasaway

Burn Baby Burn

Across the lake the foliage floated by on an early autumn breeze;
Up in the trees the colors were starting to change in all of the
leaves.

Red, gold, yellow, orange and so many variations could be seen;
All set against a cobalt blue sky and pines of dark green.

This once was her favorite time of the year feeling the brisk breeze
in the air;
Now it was just a reflection of what had been, when she hadn't a
care.

It seems her dreams were floating by just like the leaves from the
trees;
How had it all gone so wrong she wondered how he could just up
and leave?

For thirty-five years they had been together through thick and
thin;
Why now did he choose to throw it all away and just give in?

She'd heard it happening to others over the years;
Never did she believe that it would be her crying those same tears.

She now felt so very alone and faced with starting a brand new
life;
For all those many years she'd been a mother and devoted wife.

How to begin again and start a new life she wondered in her mind;
She hadn't even been on a date in such a very long time.

But begin again she did and is now happier than ever before;
Sometimes you just need to be patient as God will always open
another door.

When your days seem so dark and gloomy and you don't know
where to turn;
Let go and let God and let the past along with that bridge just burn
baby burn.

~~~

Fear thou not; for I am with thee: be not dismayed; for I am thy God: I will strengthen thee; yea, I will help thee; yea, I will uphold thee with the right hand of my righteousness. Isaiah 41:10

But the God of all grace, who hath called us unto his eternal glory by Christ Jesus, after that ye have suffered a while, make you perfect, establish, strengthen, settle you. 1 Peter 5:10

These things I have spoken unto you, that in me ye might have peace. In the world ye shall have tribulation: but be of good cheer; I have overcome the world. John 16:33

Now faith is the substance of things hoped for, the evidence of things not seen. Hebrews 11:1

I can do all things through Christ which strengthened me. Philippians 4:13

I have fought a good fight, I have finished my course, I have kept the faith: 2 Timothy 4:7

For I know the plans I have for you, declares the LORD, plans for welfare and not for evil, to give you a future and a hope. Jeremiah 29:11

Ask, and it shall be given you; seek, and ye shall find; knock, and it shall be opened unto you: Matthew 7:7

When you pass through the waters, I will be with you; and when you pass through the rivers, they will not sweep over you. When you walk through the fire, you will not be burned; the flames will not set you ablaze. Isaiah 43:2

Michael Gasaway

The Cowboy Way

Just a young girl with golden hair and bright blue eyes;
That golden palomino had been her birthday surprise.

Her cowboy grandpa knew of her dream that she held deep inside;
So he took it upon himself to show this 'lil cowgirl how to really
ride.

They spent hours together as he showed her the real cowboy
ways;
Not only how to ride but also how to care for her horse she named
Blaze.

How to muck the stalls and love and feed Blaze just right;
Brush his coat and mane and to pray for him every night.

They grew up together that horse and her you could say;
Now they run the circuit chasing barrels in a horse and rider
musical ballet.

Her cowboy grandpa cheers her on every time win or lose;
He taught her how to run for it all each time and never just cruise.

Soon she and Blaze will run in Vegas beneath those bright lights;
And yes cowboy grandpa is by their side and filled with such
delight.

Gold buckles and trophies filled the shelves as with her dream she
stayed;
She always gives thanks to God and her cowboy grandpa for
showing her the cowboy way.

~~~

Train up a child in the way he should go: and when she is old, she will not depart from it. Proverbs 22:6

Lo, children are a heritage of the LORD: and the fruit of the womb is his reward. Psalm 127:3

That the man of God may be competent, equipped for every good work. 2 Timothy 3:17

Even a child is known by his doings, whether his work be pure, and whether it be right. Proverbs 20:11

I will instruct thee and teach thee in the way which thou shalt go: I will guide thee with mine eye. Psalm 32:8

And whatsoever ye do, do it heartily, as to the Lord, and not unto men; Colossians 3:23

Whatsoever thy hand findeth to do, do it with thy might; Ecclesiastes 9:10

Delight thyself also in the LORD: and he shall give thee the desires of thine heart. Psalm 37:4

She Rides Into Tomorrow

The cotton candy clouds floating on high reflected in her dazzling
green eyes;
Once again she was faced with another case of wondering why?

Why did things seem to get so topsy-turvy in her life at times?
How had it happened again she wondered in her mind?

Remembering the poem she had once read about "how life's not
fair";
How to cowgirl up and just let the wind blow through her long dark
hair.

Let Gods wind blow all your troubles away as you take another of
life's rides;
Yes time to cowgirl up girl and let go, putting all your cares and
troubles aside.

Let go and let God handle all your cares and worries you carry
about;
Trust in His word and that He will see you through without any
doubt.

Her lovely smile is now back gracing her beautiful face;
Inside she feels Gods understanding peace and amazing grace.

Now she sits tall in the saddle with her head held high;
She rides into tomorrow, knowing that God and her friend are
always by her side.

~~~

The righteous cry out, and the Lord hears them; he delivers them from all their troubles. The Lord is close to the brokenhearted and saves those who are crushed in spirit. The righteous person may have many troubles, but the Lord delivers him from them all; Psalm 34:17-19

do not be anxious about anything, but in everything by prayer and supplication with thanksgiving let your requests be made known to God. 7 And the peace of God, which surpasses all understanding, will guard your hearts and your minds in Christ Jesus. Philippians 4:6-7

Blessed is the one who perseveres under trial because, having stood the test, that person will receive the crown of life that the Lord has promised to those who love him. James 1:12

Casting all your anxieties on him, because he cares for you. 1 Peter 5:7

Now faith is the substance of things hoped for, the evidence of things not seen. Hebrews 11:1

Delight thyself also in the LORD: and he shall give thee the desires of thine heart. Psalm 37:4

The Move

Time had moved on and now it was time for her to do the same;
It had been quite a struggle for years, but with God's help she
overcame.

As she packed memories came flooding back from happier times
she'd spent;
Memories of her children growing up made her smile, no longer
recalling the years of torment.

A single tear crept out of her emerald green eyes and rolled down
her cheek;
Yes it was time to really move on in life and for her a new future to
seek.

The decision she had made was not easy but in her heart she knew
it was right;
Knowing it wouldn't be easy but she also knew that her past she
couldn't rewrite.

All the boxes were packed and soon the movers would be there to
load;
Then it would really be time to actually move on and travel down
this new road.

Locking the door for the last time a smile crossed her beautiful
face;
Then she felt a peace within her heart and was overcome with
God's amazing grace.

Years have gone by and her life has become better than she could
ever dream;
Now instead of out of fear, it was for joy and happiness that made
her want to scream.

Put away your doubts and fears that you have faced in the past,
along with all the strife;
Sometimes you just have to let go of the past and move on with
your life.

The future is where you belong and need to move, letting God lead
and direct your way;

He will never forsake you but will guide you to a bright and beautiful new day.

It's never easy to move on in life and seek a new future down the trail;
But it's the only way that you will ever find peace, love and happiness and as you travail.

~~~

The LORD is near to the brokenhearted and saves the crushed in spirit. Psalm 34:18

Cast thy burden upon the LORD, and he shall sustain thee: he shall never suffer the righteous to be moved. Psalm 55:22

For I know the plans I have for you," declares the LORD, "plans to prosper you and not to harm you, plans to give you hope and a future. Jeremiah 29:11

Is anyone among you suffering? Let him pray. Is anyone cheerful? Let him sing praise. James 5:13

I can do all things through Christ which strengthened me. Philippians 4:13

Delight thyself also in the LORD: and he shall give thee the desires of thine heart. Psalm 37:4

For the Spirit God gave us does not make us timid, but gives us power, love and self-discipline. 2 Timothy 1:7

Rejoicing in hope; patient in tribulation; continuing instant in prayer; Romans 12:12

Michael Gasaway

Brand New Day

The day is upon me that I knew would arrive;
Now it's time to move forward and no longer just survive.

It's been a long journey this is so very true;
But now I look forward to a future bright with skies so blue.

Behind me is the past and that is where it will stay;
God has given me a fresh beginning, a brand new day.

My future I can now see shinning bright as the sun;
I can see myself laughing, loving and once again having fun.

It is the future that I had always dreamed it would be;
How was I to know that all along it was up to me.

In this moment it is so very clear like the words that I write;
This new life I see in the distant shimmering so bright.

Giving thanks to God above and praise to thee;
It was He that has led me to my real destiny.

Never have I felt so alive about what I do each day;
It fills me with happiness and joy, what can I say.

This new life, that God has given me and set me free;
Is more than I could ever imagine or expected to ever see.

My faith held strong and I trusted God even when it looked like the
end;
But He was always there with me through thick and thin.

So hang in there and don't despair and always look to God up
above;
He is always with you and will surround you with His perfect love.

~~~

For I know the plans I have for you, declares the Lord, plans for welfare and not for evil, to give you a future and a hope.
Jeremiah 29:11

For the vision is yet for an appointed time, but at the end it shall speak, and not lie: though it tarry, wait for it; because it will surely come, it will not tarry. Habakkuk 2:3

The Lord will fulfill his purpose for me; your steadfast love, O Lord, endures forever. Do not forsake the work of your hands.
Psalm 138:8

And all things, whatsoever ye shall ask in prayer, believing, ye shall receive. Matthew 21:22

These things have I spoken unto you, that my joy might remain in you, and that your joy might be full. John 15:11

But without faith it is impossible to please him: for he that cometh to God must believe that he is, and that he is a rewarder of them that diligently seek him. Hebrews 11:6

Trust in the Lord with all thine heart; and lean not unto thine own understanding. In all thy ways acknowledge him, and he shall direct thy paths. Proverbs 3:5-6

Thou wilt show me the path of life: in thy presence is fullness of joy; at thy right hand there are pleasures for evermore.
Psalm 16:11

Michael Gasaway

In Her Dreams

In her dreams she is taken back in time to that special place;
She rides along the beach on a white horse feeling the wind in her
face.

It's just a dream that she has on some of those lonely nights;
Remembering back as a young girl at the Abby, how going to the
ocean had filled her with delight.

Her dark hair glistens in the noon day sun as her eyes sparkle and
shine;
What joy her heart feels as that special memory takes her back in
time.

Smelling the ocean breeze as it touches and coats her delicate
face;
Beneath her feet she feels the warm sand as well as God's
presence and grace.

No longer a child and thousands of miles and an ocean away from
her home;
Inside she still carries a special loneliness and at times feels so
alone.

This dream she still holds dear and carries deep in her heart
within;
To find that one chivalrous knight that can stand tall and be
respected by all men.

Each and every day she prays for others but occasionally for
herself as well;
That one day that special gentleman would come and take her
away off love's carousel.

Never will she give up, doubt or fear as her faith in God is that
strong;
One day she knows that her special man and heart's desire will
come along.

Always keep your dreams alive and each day do perceive and
believe;
As God does answer all prayers in His time and as you're ready to
receive.

76

∾∾∾

But the fruit of the Spirit is love, joy, peace, patience, kindness, goodness, faithfulness, Galatians 5:22

Count it all joy, my brothers, when you meet trials of various kinds, James 1:2

And he said, "My presence will go with you, and I will give you rest." Exodus 33:14

You will seek me and find me, when you seek me with all your heart. Jeremiah 29:13

Fear not, for I am with you; be not dismayed, for I am your God; I will strengthen you, I will help you, I will uphold you with my righteous right hand. Isaiah 41:10

Casting all your anxieties on him, because he cares for you. 1 Peter 5:7

Delight yourself in the LORD, and he will give you the desires of your heart. Psalm 37:4

And let us not grow weary of doing good, for in due season we will reap, if we do not give up. Galatians 6:9

For I know the thoughts that I think toward you, saith the LORD, thoughts of peace, and not of evil, to give you an expected end. Jeremiah 29:11

Fear thou not; for I am with thee: be not dismayed; for I am thy God: I will strengthen thee; yea, I will help thee; yea, I will uphold thee with the right hand of my righteousness. Isaiah 41:10

Life's Calamities

Just when you think your life is all planned and you're future is as
bright as can be;
Everything just seems to transform as you're faced with a new
challenging adversity.

Life can hit you hard at times and knock you down to your very
knees;
Remember that God is always with you and will deliver you through
all life's calamities.

When those dark memories come breaking into your mind like a
thief in the night;
Don't give them space to expand and know that your future will
again be so bright.

Now is not the time to give up on chasing your dreams or believing
in your heart's desire;
Sometimes out of the coldness of adversity comes a new future full
of passions fire.

Forward into the future you must go and give it all you have to
give;
It's your life and it's truly up to your faith as in the end how you'll
live.

Your life can be like a rollercoaster ride at times as it throws you all
about;
Just keep moving forward even if at times you just want to scream
and shout.

One day in God's perfect timing the dark clouds will part and blue
sky you'll see;
The dreams and desires you believed in are now ready for you to
achieve.

Thank God for leading and guiding you past the dark valleys you've
gone through;
You're now at your new beginning that God has always been
preparing just for you.

So straighten up that Stetson upon your head and grab hold of
life's reins and don't be denied;

Rising with the dawn your new life is beginning and off into tomorrow you'll ride.

~~~

We are troubled on every side, yet not distressed; we are perplexed, but not in despair; Persecuted, but not forsaken; cast down, but not destroyed; 2 Corinthians 4:8-9

But the God of all grace, who hath called us unto his eternal glory by Christ Jesus, after that ye have suffered a while, make you perfect, establish, strengthen, settle you.1 Peter 5:10

I know how to be brought low, and I know how to abound. In any and every circumstance, I have learned the secret of facing plenty and hunger, abundance and need. I can do all things through him who strengthens me. Philippians 4:12-13

And all things, whatsoever ye shall ask in prayer, believing, ye shall receive. Matthew 21:22

Let us not become weary in doing good, for at the proper time we will reap a harvest if we do not give up. Galatians 6:9

For I know the plans I have for you, declares the LORD, plans for welfare and not for evil, to give you a future and a hope. Jeremiah 29:11

Behold, I will do a new thing; now it shall spring forth; shall ye not know it? I will even make a way in the wilderness, and rivers in the desert. Isaiah 43:19

Delight thyself also in the LORD: and he shall give thee the desires of thine heart. Psalm 37:4

Michael Gasaway

Sands of Time

There she sits waiting for me in the sands of time;
When once again together I'll be hers and she'll be mine.

She's more beautiful than I remember when the earthly fields
together we walked hand n' hand;
Her beauty has been transcended with a heavenly glow that is so
grand.

No more tears or pain will we feel in our hearts;
Just a pure love for each other that will never depart.

Time will have no meaning as forever each day we'll spend;
Beyond the earthly bounds into heaven we will transcend.

Beautiful heavenly scenes we will collectively view with love;
It will be so grand as we spend eternity together above.

God once blessed us on earth with a special love so pure and true;
Now we'll spend together forever, never more to bid each other
adieu.

~~~

'He will wipe every tear from their eyes. There will be no more death' or mourning or crying or pain, for the old order of things has passed away." Revelation 21:4

Love is patient and kind; love does not envy or boast; it's not arrogant or rude. It does not insist on its own way; it is not irritable or resentful; it does not rejoice at wrongdoing, but rejoices with the truth. Love bears all things, believes all things, hopes all things, endures all things. Love never ends.
1 Corinthians 13:4-8

But as it is written, Eye hath not seen, nor ear heard, neither have entered into the heart of man, the things which God hath prepared for them that love him. 1 Corinthians 2:9

And above all these put on love, which binds everything together in perfect harmony. Colossians 3:14

Michael Gasaway

One Last Ride

About women cowboys do sometimes sit and ponder;
A woman's actions and words do at times just make them wonder.

Seemingly to speak in another language, all of their own;
They leave many a mystified cowboy, like they have just been thrown.

Try as they might some cowboys keep giving it another try;
They never give up and keep looking for that one last ride.

A last ride that this time with all their might they will cleave;
To that special woman's heart and true love they will achieve.

Praying that this will be the last first ride of their life;
That in the end the love of their life will become his wife.

Not another gold buckle does he this time want to win;
But a gold ring on her finger and a true love never to end.

One last ride that will go on forever in time;
Just like the words in that 'ole cowboy poets rhyme.

~~~

And the LORD God said, It is not good that the man should be alone; I will make him an help meet for him. Genesis 2:18

An excellent wife who can find? She is far more precious than jewels. Proverbs 31:10

But seek ye first the kingdom of God, and his righteousness; and all these things shall be added unto you. Matthew 6:33

And let us not grow weary of doing good, for in due season we will reap, if we do not give up. Galatians 6:9

For I know the plans I have for you," declares the LORD, "plans to prosper you and not to harm you, plans to give you hope and a future. Jeremiah 29:11

May he grant you your heart's desire and fulfill all your plans! Psalm 20:4

Michael Gasaway

LIFE'S TEST

Appear to be that which you desire to become;
Be that which is more than your average sum.

In all that you attempt, strive to do your best;
Only then will you be able to pass life's test.

Always look to the sunrise and what it might bring;
For with the dawn of each day brings forth a new song to sing.

Live each new day as if it were your last here to be;
For tomorrow is not promised to you or to me.

Do what is right each day and live without regret;
Then you can smile and rejoice with each sunset.

Some days may test you down to your very soul;
But just know that God is always with you, young or old.

Remember the teacher is always silent when the test is given;
Each test will help show you how you should be livin'.

When each trial is complete and your ready to move on in life;
Give thanks to God as He will lead and direct you through all strife.

Now go forward with a smile having past another life's test this
day;
How you live your life will decide your next quest along life's
Highway.

~~~

Do your best to present yourself to God as one approved, a worker who has no need to be ashamed, rightly handling the word of truth. 2 Timothy 2:15

Finally, brothers, whatever is true, whatever is honorable, whatever is just, whatever is pure, whatever is lovely, whatever is commendable, if there is any excellence, if there is anything worthy of praise, think about these things. Philippians 4:8

And we know that for those who love God all things work together for good, for those who are called according to his purpose. Romans 8:28

Blessed is the man who remains steadfast under trial, for when he has stood the test he will receive the crown of life, which God has promised to those who love him. James 1:12

No temptation has overtaken you that is not common to man. God is faithful, and he will not let you be tempted beyond your ability, but with the temptation he will also provide the way of escape, that you may be able to endure it. 1 Corinthians 10:13

But understand this that in the last days there will come times of difficulty. 2 Timothy 3:1

Michael Gasaway

Love's Carousel

Around and around each night and day she just seems to go;
Feeling trapped on love's carousel like a wild eyed doe.

I've heard it said, if you keep doing the identical thing then the
results will be the same;
If you don't change your ways in time it may just drive you insane.

People all over want that one special person with their life to share;
Traveling through the years together with that one singular love,
living life without a care.

Unfortunately life doesn't work that way at least not in the time
and ways we planned;
Most give up and just settle or walk away before reaching their
own promise land.

Sometimes we are the ones that need to change our actions, words
and deeds;
You have to prepare yourself and align your heart and mind in
order to receive.

Trust in God and ask Him to lead, guide and direct your steps each
day;
Don't give up when you grow weary or the pace seems too slow
along the way.

One day in the not too distant future as all is aligned from heaven
above;
You'll jump off love's carousel into the arms of your one true love.

So don't give up on working hard at being the person God created
you to be;
You'll look back one day and realize it was your choices that made
it hard or easy to fulfill your destiny.

Now put a smile on your face and start making those changes, you
know the ones;
The sooner your complete each task the sooner your destiny and
true love will come.

~~~

No temptation has overtaken you that is not common to man. God is faithful, and he will not let you be tempted beyond your ability, but with the temptation he will also provide the way of escape, that you may be able to endure it. 1 Corinthians 10:13

For God gave us a spirit not of fear but of power and love and self-control. 2 Timothy 1:7

And be not conformed to this world: but be ye transformed by the renewing of your mind, that ye may prove what is that good, and acceptable, and perfect, will of God. Romans 12:2

Do not be anxious about anything, but in every situation, by prayer and petition, with thanksgiving, present your requests to God. And the peace of God, which transcends all understanding, will guard your hearts and your minds in Christ Jesus. Philippians 4:6-7

And let us not grow weary of doing good, for in due season we will reap, if we do not give up. Galatians 6:9

Be ye strong therefore, and let not your hands be weak: for your work shall be rewarded. 2 Chronicles 15:7

Delight thyself also in the LORD: and he shall give thee the desires of thine heart. Psalm 37:4

But as it is written, Eye hath not seen, nor ear heard, neither have entered into the heart of man, the things which God hath prepared for them that love him. 1 Corinthians 2:9

For I know the thoughts that I think toward you, saith the LORD, thoughts of peace, and not of evil, to give you an expected end. Jeremiah 29:11

Michael Gasaway

Never Alone

Being alone is not as bad or even lonesome as it once was for me;
For truly alone, today or tomorrow I know that I will never be.

You'll never leave me or forsake me when trouble does appear;
You're always standing there with me so that I will have no fear.

No matter how far down that I may stumble and fall;
You're always there to help me up again and once again give me
your all.

When in need I don't have to worry if you'll show up like some
friends;
On you, I know that forever I can and will always depend.

Soon I'll travel on with a smile on my face;
For now I know that you're always with me, and I will forever feel
your amazing grace.

With no fear or worry of what tomorrow may or may not bring;
On I will go with a song in my heart that for you I do sing.

I awake with joy in my heart at the dawn of each new day;
Knowing that you are with me no matter what may come my way.

Thank you for guiding me through all the years;
Thank you for being there in my pain and to help wipe away the
many tears.

It's been a long beautiful journey that I have for so many years
traveled along;
Some days were sad, but most were happy and filled with such
wondrous song.

So down the road I travel but now I'm never truly all alone;
For I now know that at the end of Life's Highway you'll pick me up
and carry me home.

~~~

Let your conversation be without covetousness; and be content with such things as ye have: for he hath said, I will never leave thee, nor forsake thee. Hebrews 13:5

Casting all your care upon him; for he cares for you. 1 Peter 5:7

For the LORD *will not forsake his people for his great name's sake: because it hath pleased the* LORD *to make you his people. 1 Samuel 12:22*

But the Lord is with me as a dread warrior; therefore my persecutors will stumble; they will not overcome me. They will be greatly shamed, for they will not succeed. Their eternal dishonor will never be forgotten. Jeremiah 20:11

You have put more joy in my heart more than they have when their grain and wine abound. Psalm 4:7

And God shall wipe away all tears from their eyes; and there shall be no more death, neither sorrow, nor crying, neither shall there be any more pain: for the former things are passed away. Revelation 21:4

For I know the plans I have for you, declares the Lord, plans for welfare and not for evil, to give you a future and a hope. Jeremiah 29:11

But as it is written, Eye hath not seen, nor ear heard, neither have entered into the heart of man, the things which God hath prepared for them that love him. 1 Corinthians 2:9

Fear

Sometimes we allow fear to just take control;
Instead of trusting in God and just letting it go.

Fear, real or imaginary can be so debilitating it seems;
Don't allow it to invade and destroy your dreams.

It has no place in your life and especially not in your heart;
So send the devil packing as of fear he is a part.

Put your faith and trust in God up on high;
Banish fear and worry from your heart and say goodbye.

God will lead, guide and direct your steps each day;
It's up to you to ask and allow God to show you the way.

Keep ever vigilant of the devil and his many schemes;
Remember God is always with you and reigns supreme.

So put that smile on your face and expel fear from your life;
Trust that God will always walk with you through any strife.

Then one day to heaven you'll go with God to spend;
There to live in glory with no worries or troubles to contend.

~~~

Fear thou not; for I am with thee: be not dismayed; for I am thy God: I will strengthen thee; yea, I will help thee; yea, I will uphold thee with the right hand of my righteousness. Isaiah 41:10

For God hath not given us the spirit of fear; but of power, and of love, and of a sound mind. 2 Timothy 1:7

I sought the LORD, and he answered me and delivered me from all my fears. Psalm 34:4

When I am afraid, I put my trust in you. In God, whose word I praise, in God I trust; I shall not be afraid. What can flesh do to me? Psalm 56:3-4

Have not I commanded thee? Be strong and of a good courage; be not afraid, neither be thou dismayed: for the LORD thy God is with thee whithersoever thou goest. Joshua 1:9

Yea, though I walk through the valley of the shadow of death, I will fear no evil: for thou art with me; thy rod and thy staff they comfort me. Psalm 23:4

Michael Gasaway

New Beginning

It's a new day and it is crisp and clear;
The new beginning God promised her is almost here.

She can hardly wait for her new expectations to see;
Just like a child that is waiting on Christmas Eve.

Her journey is now at an end and her future will soon begin;
Now she's looking forward to really living life once again.

It will be all that she has ever wanted or dreamed it could be;
In her mind she can see it ever so clearly.

All that was lost or taken is in the past now;
But God's redemption will restore them somehow.

Can't explain how that she knows other than the Bible says it's so;
Now she looks ahead and forward into tomorrow she must go.

With a smile on her face that comes from deep within;
This is the day that she will really start living again.

It is so good to feel this much alive;
But even better is to know that these feeling come from deep
inside.

From deep inside these feelings one day started to grow;
At first she didn't really understand but now she truly knows.

Thank you God she prays for the road that she's now taken;
And for always being with her as never was she ever forsaken.

The lessons she had learned have been hard at times and came
with a high price to pay;
In the end they were worth the cost for the future she sees coming
her way.

So now through the open door with the morning light she boldly
will ride;
She'll ride into tomorrow following her destiny riding with God by
her side.

≈≈≈

It is of the Lord's mercies that we are not consumed, because his compassions fail not. They are new every morning: great is thy faithfulness. Lamentations 3:22-23

Therefore if any man be in Christ, he is a new creature: old things are passed away; behold, all things are become new. 2 Corinthians 5:17

For God gave us a spirit not of fear but of power and love and self-control. 2 Timothy 1:7

But my God shall supply all your need according to his riches in glory by Christ Jesus. Philippians 4:19

"Therefore do not be anxious about tomorrow, for tomorrow will be anxious for itself. Sufficient for the day is its own trouble." Matthew 6:34

Fear thou not; for I am with thee: be not dismayed; for I am thy God: I will strengthen thee; yea, I will help thee; yea, I will uphold thee with the right hand of my righteousness. Isaiah 41:10

But when he, the Spirit of truth, comes, he will guide you into all the truth. He will not speak on his own; he will speak only what he hears, and he will tell you what is yet to come. John 16:13

Trust in the LORD with all your heart and lean not on your own understanding; in all your ways submit to him, and he will make your paths straight. Proverbs 3:5-6

So now faith, hope, and love abide, these three; but the greatest of these is love. 1 Corinthians 13:13

Alone or Lonely

She couldn't stand to be alone as she traveled through life;
From relationship to relationship she went wondering why she was
always in so much emotional strife.

Seeming to settle rather than waiting for the right one to come
along;
Wandering through life trying to figure out why each relationship
did go so wrong.

Each time the loneliness crept in and the circle began again;
Round and round she goes and wonders how this time it will end.

Why she prays to God, does it always seem to end in the same
way;
But she never really stops and listens to what God has to say.

Most of the time it's better to stay alone than be lonely later and
feel the pain;
If you never learn from the past then you will never really see any
gain.

So never settle or lower your standards or let your beliefs become
swayed;
For if you do, then one day your true heart's desire will become
betrayed.

Take your time and let God have the lead as you travel down life's
trail;
Keep your complete trust in God and the next time you will not fail.

Turn your life over to God and let Him be your one true guide;
Then you'll find that one special person and together through life
you'll ride.

~~~

Wait on the LORD: be of good courage, and he shall strengthen thine heart: wait, I say, on the LORD. Psalm 27:14

For still the vision awaits its appointed time; it hastens to the end— it will not lie. If it seems slow, wait for it; it will surely come; it will not delay. Habakkuk 2:3

Delight thyself also in the LORD: and he shall give thee the desires of thine heart. Psalm 37:4

Fear thou not; for I am with thee: be not dismayed; for I am thy God: I will strengthen thee; yea, I will help thee; yea, I will uphold thee with the right hand of my righteousness. Isaiah 41:10

Create in me a clean heart, O God; and renew a right spirit within me. Psalm 51:10

Do not be anxious about anything, but in every situation, by prayer and petition, with thanksgiving, present your requests to God. And the peace of God, which transcends all understanding, will guard your hearts and your minds in Christ Jesus. Philippians 4:6-7

And let us not grow weary of doing good, for in due season we will reap, if we do not give up. Galatians 6:9

I will instruct thee and teach thee in the way which thou shall go: I will guide thee with mine eye. Psalm 32:8

Michael Gasaway

God's Signs

We see the signs everyday as we travel down the road;
Some say stop, one way, caution, slow and others say go.

But when it comes to life's roadways we tend to ignore the signs;
They are God's warnings, and given to us as guidelines.

We all have 20/20 vision when it comes to poignant hindsight;
But only with emotional bliss and in the moment do we delight.

Then comes that faithful day, when it all falls apart;
You are left wondering what happened, with a broken heart.

We then find ourselves in such disturbing stress;
We look to God and ask how He led us into such a mess.

God just smiles and shakes His head in wonder;
How big do His signs have to be, until you discover?

But in time discover we do, and God's lessons we learn;
Then you're free to travel on, without regret or concern.

Sometimes you have to turn around in order to start again;
Repair those fences and make amends, then you can truly begin.

So don't ignore those warning signs as you travel life's road.
God put them there, so you'd know which way to go.

Always ask God to lead and guide your steps each day;
Then trust in His word as he leads and guides you along life's
highway.

~~~

God also testified to it by signs, wonders and various miracles, and by gifts of the Holy Spirit distributed according to his will.
Hebrews 2:4

In all thy ways acknowledge him, and he shall direct thy paths.
Proverbs 3:6

"Tell us, when will these things be, and what will be the sign when all these things are about to be accomplished?" Mark 13:4

So Jesus said to him, "Unless you see signs and wonders you will not believe." John 4:48

This man came to Jesus by night and said to him, "Rabbi, we know that you are a teacher come from God, for no one can do these signs that you do unless God is with him." John 3:2

A man's heart devises' his way: but the LORD *directed his steps.*
Proverbs 16:9

For I know the thoughts that I think toward you, saith the LORD, *thoughts of peace, and not of evil, to give you an expected end.*
Jeremiah 29:11

Take Time

Looking up at the sky above, she couldn't remember it ever looking
so blue;
Colorful leaves seemed to stand out as she took in this magnificent
view.

It had been a tough year as many of them had been in her recent
past;
The loss of someone special can do that filling you with a pain that
just seems to last.

Wondering each day if happiness and a new life she'll ever get to
begin;
Awakening day after day she prays that God will help her to go
forward again.

Some days she seems to fall deeper into that abyss of despair and
pain;
Falling deeper and deeper she can't help but wonder if she'll ever
be the same.

Loss can take many shapes and forms as you travel facing life's
strife;
It can be the loss of love or maybe the unexplainable loss of
someone's life.

It's never easy to understand why God allows things to happen in
this way;
You just try to understand and trust that God will give you peace
one day.

Take time to heal and allow God to open your eyes so a brighter
future you'll see;
Then one day your outlook will be brighter than you ever imagined
it could be.

Time has slowly marched on and healing has taken hold of her
heart;
Her expectations are brighter now as she has let God give her a
brand new start.

She will never forget and always remember the happy times they
shared together;

98

It was her faith and trust in God that moved her forward able to withstand any weather.

Remember this story and put your trust and faith in God above; He will always be with you and lead and guide you with His unconditional and merciful love.

~~~

And God shall wipe away all tears from their eyes; and there shall be no more death, neither sorrow, nor crying, neither shall there be any more pain: for the former things are passed away.
Revelation 21:4

For I reckon that the sufferings of this present time are not worthy to be compared with the glory which shall be revealed in us.
Romans 8:18

The night racks my bones, and the pain that gnaws me takes no rest. Job 30:17

For I know the plans I have for you," declares the LORD, "plans to prosper you and not to harm you, plans to give you hope and a future. Jeremiah 29:11

Trust in the Lord with all thine heart; and lean not unto thine own understanding. In all thy ways acknowledge him, and he shall direct thy paths. Proverbs 3:5-6

Teach me to do your will, for you are my God! Let your good Spirit lead me on level ground! Psalm 143:10

Heal me, O LORD, and I shall be healed; save me, and I shall be saved: for thou art my praise. Jeremiah 17:14

Michael Gasaway

Pain and Anguish

They carry it with them and sometimes way down deep;
It's a constant pain and anguish when relief is what they seek.

Some days they just go through the motions trying to get by;
Then at times they just want to give up and die.

The pain can lead to addictions as spiraling deeper down they sink;
Sometimes they reach for pills or that bottle and another stiff drink.

It's not the life they chose or the one they really wish;
But it's the one served to them so cold upon life's dish.

Many try to break the addictions demons that have grabbed hold;
Try as they might many are pulled back down deep and controlled.

There are some that break free from these chains in time;
It takes an inner strength, a true friend, outside help and God to make that climb.

So reach out for a friend and climb out from the abyss you have sank;
Then one day you'll look to heaven and to those that helped and God you'll want to thank.

~~~

And God shall wipe away all tears from their eyes; and there shall be no more death, neither sorrow, nor crying, neither shall there be any more pain: Revelation 21:4

For I reckon that the sufferings of this present time are not worthy to be compared with the glory which shall be revealed in us. Romans 8:18

And we know that all things work together for good to them that love God, to them who are the called according to his purpose. Romans 8:28

There hath no temptation taken you but such as is common to man: but God is faithful, who will not suffer you to be tempted above that ye are able; but will with the temptation also make a way to escape, that ye may be able to bear it. 1 Corinthians 10:13

Let us break their bands asunder, and cast away their cords from us. Psalm 2:3

The LORD is my strength and my shield; in him my heart trusts, and I am helped; my heart exults, and with my song I give thanks to him. Psalm 28:7

Michael Gasaway

Pain Filled Days

The pain she lived with had gone on now for so very long;
It just seemed to play over and over like a really bad song.

Some days were a cloudless azure blue filled with sunshine and
hope;
Then there were those pain filled days that made it difficult to even
cope.

Round n' round yet to another doctor trying and make sense of it
all inside;
But on those dark nights the deeper into depression she did slide.

Trying not to use the pain killers except on those really bad days;
She never liked the way it seemed to put her into a drug induced
haze.

Like so many woman and men they find themselves in such strife;
Some just give up or completely give in to the drugs giving up on
life.

It's not easy to fight this pain day after day feeling so alone and
blue;
But never give up as God is always there and will see you through.

Just keep believing and trusting in God in heaven above;
One day your painful prayers will be answered by God with love.

Til' that day keep praying and trusting doing the best you can;
One day the dark clouds will give way to blue and you'll be forever
pain free again.

~~~

For I reckon that the sufferings of this present time are not worthy to be compared with the glory which shall be revealed in us. Romans 8:18

The night racks my bones, and the pain that gnaws me takes no rest. Job 30:17

For I know the plans I have for you," declares the LORD, "plans to prosper you and not to harm you, plans to give you hope and a future. Jeremiah 29:11

Fear thou not; for I am with thee: be not dismayed; for I am thy God: I will strengthen thee; yea, I will help thee; yea, I will uphold thee with the right hand of my righteousness. Isaiah 41:10

But Jesus beheld them, and said unto them, With men this is impossible; but with God all things are possible. Matthew 19:26

And let us not grow weary of doing good, for in due season we will reap, if we do not give up. Galatians 6:9

Likewise the Spirit helps us in our weakness. For we do not know what to pray for as we ought, but the Spirit himself intercedes for us with groanings too deep for words. Romans 8:26

Michael Gasaway

A Cowboy's Life

Many a trail he had traveled chasing steers from South Texas to
those Kansas plains;
Some parts were so very hot and dusty and then there were those
damn 'ole rains.

He had lost count of how many drives he had ridden pushing cattle
north of the line;
Never would he forget the many hands he'd ridden with sharing
good and bad times.

This would be his last drive as things were changing as times
moved on;
Back down to Texas he'd head and try to find a new life with
tomorrow's dawn.

A cowboy's life is all he really knew and it was the life he dearly
loved;
There was nothing better in his mind than out under the stars, just
him and God above.

Sometimes he thought of her and the happy times they had shared
together;
Often he wondered if she'd share his cowboy life standing with him
against all weather.

Having saved up from many a herd over the years plus the bonus
from the last drive;
Now he thought was the time to buy that little spread and give love
and marriage a try.

It would be the best of both worlds, still a cowboy but with that
lady by his side;
She said yes and a new life they did begin, as faith, love and
destiny did collide.

Now many generations have passed on down the line and the
acreage has multiplied;
From humble beginnings the cowboy and the lady created a ranch
that now took a day to ride.

Doing what you truly love with the person you dearly love by your side;
That is the secret of true happiness as off into the sunset together you ride.

~~~

And whatsoever ye do, do it heartily, as to the Lord, and not unto men; Colossians 3:23

Do your best to present yourself to God as one approved, a worker who has no need to be ashamed, rightly handling the word of truth. 2 Timothy 2:15

Prepare your work outside; get everything ready for yourself in the field, Proverbs 24:27

Be sure you know the condition of your flocks, give careful attention to your herds; Proverbs 27:23

I thank God whom I serve, as did my ancestors, with a clear conscience, as I remember you constantly in my prayers night and day. 2 Timothy 1:3

An excellent wife who can find? She is far more precious than jewels. Proverbs 31:10

Delight yourself in the LORD, and he will give you the desires of your heart. Psalm 37:4

I perceived that there is nothing better for them than to be joyful and to do good as long as they live; Ecclesiastes 3:12

Why

There are times in our lives when we want to shout that word to
the sky;
At times of loneliness and helplessness that to God we want to cry
out, why?

It often comes at the darkest hour of our lives that we may ever
see;
The loss of a loved one struck down in their prime that we can't
except or believe.

This most often is the time we cry out to God up above;
We feel numb, dazed and confused and so want to again feel their
love.

Answers we seek from God as to why this terrible thing did befall
our loved one;
But no answers ever come from a senseless act when all is said
and done.

As the days go by we continue to try and make sense where none
can be made;
During these dark times we even question the many prayers that
we've prayed.

The days, months and years slowly move forward in time;
From the deep abyss you sank, step by step out toward the light
you climb.

Then one day the sun seems brighter and the sky an azure blue;
That's when you realize that the peace of God the Bible speaks of,
has come over you.

Everyone grieves in their own way at a different pace;
But sooner or later you must move on and get back in life's race.

Your lost loved one would want you to move forward and begin
anew;
So let today be your new beginning and know they will always be
with you.

So put a song in your heart and a smile on your face;
Let God lead, guide and direct your steps forward with His amazing grace.

~~~

These things I have spoken unto you, that in me ye might have peace. In the world ye shall have tribulation: but be of good cheer; I have overcome the world. John 16:33

And God shall wipe away all tears from their eyes; and there shall be no more death, neither sorrow, nor crying, neither shall there be any more pain: for the former things are passed away. Revelation 21:4

For whatever was written in former days was written for our instruction, that through endurance and through the encouragement of the Scriptures we might have hope. Romans 15:4

I know, O LORD, that the way of man is not in himself, that it is not in man who walks to direct his steps. Jeremiah 10:23

For I know the plans I have for you, declares the LORD, plans for welfare and not for evil, to give you a future and a hope. Jeremiah 29:11

Behold, I will do a new thing; now it shall spring forth; shall ye not know it? I will even make a way in the wilderness, and rivers in the desert. Isaiah 43:19

And of his fullness have all we received, and grace for grace. John 1:16

Michael Gasaway

Mysteries of Love

She didn't fully understand the mysteries of love and life;
Each day she prayed to God, please take away this strife.

Sometimes she asked God to send true love her way;
This was the prayer she prayed most every night and day.

In her life she had endured enough heartache and pain;
Through the years there had been too many storms and rain.

Then one day her prayer was answered from God above;
Down from heaven it seemed to come on wings of a dove.

Not seeming to make any sense to her in her mind;
Emotions had her reeling, like she had lost control this time.

The walls she had built seemed to crumble before her eyes;
Slowly she realized that before her stood loves prize.

It seems to happen when you least expect it too;
Seems so mysterious until the day it happens to you.

Your feelings will ebb and flow, just like the ocean tide;
Then into the future you boldly go with your eyes open wide.

She has found her true love and destiny and knows that it's right;
Now she looks forward to a life of true love and passionate nights.

Just keep your faith strong and keep trusting in God on high;
One day true love will find you and your heart's desire will be
satisfied.

~~~

Love is patient and kind; love does not envy or boast; it is not arrogant or rude. It does not insist on its own way; it is not irritable or resentful; it does not rejoice at wrongdoing, but rejoices with the truth. Love bears all things, believes all things, hopes all things, endures all things. 1 Corinthians 13:4-7

For I know the plans I have for you, declares the Lord, plans for welfare and not for evil, to give you a future and a hope. Jeremiah 29:11

For the vision is yet for an appointed time, but at the end it shall speak, and not lie: though it tarry, wait for it; because it will surely come, it will not tarry. Habakkuk 2:3

And after you have suffered a little while, the God of all grace, who has called you to his eternal glory in Christ, will himself restore, confirm, strengthen, and establish you. 1 Peter 5:10

The Lord will fulfill his purpose for me; your steadfast love, O Lord, endures forever. Do not forsake the work of your hands. Psalm 138:8

But without faith it is impossible to please him: for he that cometh to God must believe that he is, and that he is a rewarder of them that diligently seek him. Hebrews 11:6

Michael Gasaway

Love's Desire

The bonfire was burning; the music was playing as he drove up in
his 'ole truck;
He just needed to get away and maybe meet someone new with
any luck.

In her eyes the flames just seemed to dance and twinkle as she
watched the fire;
Captivated by her long blonde hair and smile and was suddenly hit
by loves desire.

Country music was playing and some couples were getting up to
dance;
Now was the time to boldly go over and ask her and take the
chance.

She looked up as he spoke the words and he saw the bluest eyes in
Texas looking back at him;
Yes she said and away they danced into the night all the time
wearing his cowboy grin.

Under the stars they came together on that fateful night so very
long ago;
Where had the years gone, but years of happiness with several
children they had to show.

He had built her a special fire pit many seasons ago as an
anniversary gift one year;
Many a night they sat and talked holding each other and at times
shedding a tear.

Now it was a place for family gatherings and roast marshmallows
and such;
They both viewed it as a special place that took them back in time
where they both felt loves rush.

Now alone she sits and watching the embers slowly fading into the
blackness of night;
How thankful she feels that together they had spent over 50 years
of complete delight.

In her heart she knows that together they'll be again just like the
story to her he had read;
Waiting under the heavenly oak he'll be, just like the poem is what
he had said.

Now as one for all eternity they walk the fields up upon heavens
scenes above;
Hand 'n hand they go together forever feeling theirs and Gods
eternal love.

~~~

*Love is patient and kind; love does not envy or boast; it is not
arrogant or rude. It does not insist on its own way; it is not
irritable or resentful; it does not rejoice at wrongdoing, but rejoices
with the truth. Love bears all things, believes all things, hopes all
things, and endures all things. Love never ends.
1 Corinthians 13:4-8*

*Beloved, let us love one another: for love is of God; and every one
that loves is born of God, and knows God. 1 John 4:7*

*And now these three remain: faith, hope and love. But the greatest
of these is love. 1 Corinthians 13:13*

*He who finds a wife finds a good thing and obtains favor from
the LORD. Proverbs 18:22*

*An excellent wife who can find? She is far more precious than
jewels. Proverbs 31:10*

*Husbands, love your wives, even as Christ also loved the church,
and gave himself for it; Ephesians 5:25*

Just Climb

Life's a dance and is meant to be enjoyed with each step you take;
Ask God to lead, guide and direct the steps each day you make.

Relish each day as if it were to be your very last;
Dance in the rain letting go of your painful past.

We are each given a fresh beginning with each new sunrise;
Therefore never give up on your dreams and don't ever
compromise.

God gave each of us certain dreams inside to fulfill;
So swing for the fence just to enjoy the thrill.

You'll never reach them if you don't step out on faith and hope;
Don't be satisfied with sitting on the sidelines of life just trying to
cope.

It's your life and you only get to go around one time;
Don't let that mountain in your path stop you, just climb.

It won't be easy and many dreams come with a price to pay;
Keep trusting in God above and He'll show you the way.

Then one day you'll see it right there before your eyes;
Standing in front of you is God's gift, your dream fulfilled and life's
prize.

~~~

Trust in the Lord with all thine heart; and lean not unto thine own understanding. In all thy ways acknowledge him, and he shall direct thy paths. Proverbs 3:5-6

I perceived that there is nothing better for them than to be joyful and to do good as long as they live; Ecclesiastes 3:12

And let us not grow weary of doing good, for in due season we will reap, if we do not give up. Galatians 6:9

Delight thyself also in the LORD: and he shall give thee the desires of thine heart. Psalm 37:4

For I know the plans I have for you," declares the LORD, "plans to prosper you and not to harm you, plans to give you hope and a future. Jeremiah 29:11

And without faith it is impossible to please God, because anyone who comes to him must believe that he exists and that he rewards those who earnestly seek him. Hebrews 11:6

Michael Gasaway

That Special Day

The horses were saddled and the chores we're all done;
Here she came purposely walking with a big smile as her eyes
sparkled in the sun.

He had the day all planned with the saddle bags packed with a
picnic surprise;
Up to the lake at a leisurely pace is where he planned for them to
ride.

Together they rode into the rising sun lightening their way;
What a beautiful sunrise making such a grand display.

At the lake they stopped as he leaned over kissing her sweet lips;
Climbing down he helped her holding her by her graceful hips.

The sun was glistening off the lake like diamonds in the sky;
Feeling so blessed when he held her and looked deep into her
dazzling green eyes.

They place the blanket down with some wine, meat, cheese and
fruit to eat;
Making this day for her he wanted it to be a very special treat.

They walked around hand n' hand enjoying the breeze on this
beautiful day in spring;
Then he knelt down on bended knee with a yellow rose and a shiny
ring.

"Will you marry me and do me the honor of being my wife;
I will love and cherish you always for the rest of my life".

He slipped the ring on her finger and the rest is history they say;
After 30 years of marriage they still return to that spot
remembering back to that special day.

~~~

Beloved, let us love one another: for love is of God; and every one that loves is born of God, and knows God. 1 John 4:7

An excellent wife who can find? She is far more precious than jewels. Proverbs 31:10

And now these three remain: faith, hope and love. But the greatest of these is love. 1 Corinthians 13:13

He who finds a wife finds a good thing and obtains favor from the LORD. Proverbs 18:22

Husbands, love your wives, even as Christ also loved the church, and gave himself for it; Ephesians 5:25

*Love is patient and kind; love does not envy or boast; it is not arrogant or rude. It does not insist on its own way; it is not irritable or resentful; it does not rejoice at wrongdoing, but rejoices with the truth. Love bears all things, believes all things, hopes all things, and endures all things. Love never ends.
1 Corinthians 13:4-8*

Above all, keep loving one another earnestly, since love covers a multitude of sins. 1 Peter 4:8

Delight thyself also in the LORD: and he shall give thee the desires of thine heart. Psalm 37:4

Michael Gasaway

This Same Path

She often came here so many times over the years;
It was a place of solitude where she could think and escape her
fears.

Fall had begun and was her favorite time of year to be at the lake;
Although this time she carried within the burden of a deep heart
ache.

The last year or so she had been through more than her share of
strife;
Now all alone and wondering what was to become of her life.

High above, she saw a hawk soaring against a cobalt blue sky;
Remembering back to a poem she once read and how she must
continue to try.

To never give up and to just keep moving forward and trusting in
God above;
That He would lead guide and direct her steps with His perfect
love.

Along the lake pathway she walked remembering the other poems
she'd read;
To let go of all her doubts and fears and especially her sense of
dread.

Just letting go and let God have the reins and to just truly trust
and believe;
Have faith her future would be brighter and better than she could
ever perceive.

It had been a year and back to the lake on another fall day she
came;
The air was brisk the leaves were changing and no longer did she
have a heart gone lame.

Not long after being here on that fall day just the year before;
She had met that special cowboy who opened up loves door.

Along this same path they now walked hand 'n hand together;
This love they now found with each other will withstand any
weather.

116

So keep believing and trusting in God in heaven high above;
One day you too will be riding the trail with your one true love.

~~~

*And rising very early in the morning, while it was still dark, he
departed and went out to a desolate place, and there he prayed.
Mark 1:35*

*There is no fear in love; but perfect love cast out fear: because
fear hath torment. He that fears is not made perfect in love.
1 John 4:18*

*Blessed is the man that endures temptation: for when he is tried,
he shall receive the crown of life, which the Lord hath promised to
them that love him. James 1:12*

*And let us not grow weary of doing good, for in due season we will
reap, if we do not give up. Galatians 6:9*

*Do not be anxious about anything, but in everything by prayer and
supplication with thanksgiving let your requests be made known to
God. Philippians 4:6*

*For God hath not given us the spirit of fear; but of power, and of
love, and of a sound mind. 2 Timothy 1:7*

*Delight thyself also in the LORD: and he shall give thee the desires
of thine heart. Psalm 37:4*

*Trust in the LORD with all thy heart; and lean not unto thine own
understanding. Proverbs 3:5*

117

Michael Gasaway

The Dream of True Love

Her dark hair shimmered like an eagle's wing in flight;
Brown we're her eyes that sparkled with gold and a smile so big
and bright.

The brilliant yellow sunflower she held was as bright as a
Portuguese sun;
Thinking back on her journey and remembering how it had all
begun.

Time has passed by and she wonders if true love has done the
same;
How she has dreamt of finding that special man that would kindle
the fire of loves flame.

Doubt and fear had at times made her leery and taken its toll;
But her faith has always remained strong down deep into her very
soul.

Adversity of the past would not deter her from her life's fate;
Sometimes she wondered just how long she'd have to wait.

Her voice was like that of an angel when she sang a song;
Listening to her sweet voice could make you want to sing along.

Just one of her many talents that make her such a special woman
inside;
Seeing her walk across the floor she just seems to dance and glide.

Yes a very special woman that is so very hard to find in this day
and age;
A European beauty that is comfortable either on or off the stage.

Then almost as if in a dream he appeared one star filled night;
Their eyes touched and then their hearts almost seem to jump for
delight.

They ate chestnuts as they walked through the country side a love
so true;
This dream she vowed would happen one day and with the past
she'd bid adieu.

Now into the future they walk hand n' hand with a smile on each
face;
Two lonely hearts that didn't give up, and were blessed from
above, with God's amazing grace.

~~~

*Love is patient and kind; love does not envy or boast; it is not
arrogant or rude. It does not insist on its own way; it is not
irritable or resentful; it does not rejoice at wrongdoing, but rejoices
with the truth. 1 Corinthians 13:4-6*

*For God hath not given us the spirit of fear; but of power, and of
love, and of a sound mind. 2 Timothy 1:7*

*Above all, taking the shield of faith, wherewith ye shall be able to
quench all the fiery darts of the wicked. Ephesians 6:16*

*For we wrestle not against flesh and blood, but against
principalities, against powers, against the rulers of the darkness of
this world, against spiritual wickedness in high places.
Ephesians 6:12*

*But the God of all grace, who hath called us unto his eternal glory
by Christ Jesus, after that ye have suffered a while, make you
perfect, establish, strengthen, settle you. 1 Peter 5:10*

*In all thy ways acknowledge him, and he shall direct thy paths.
Proverbs 3:6*

*May he give you the desire of your heart and make all your plans
succeed. Psalm 20:4*

Michael Gasaway

The Cowboy and the City Girl

I was a widower with five sons;
And well, experience with daughters, I really had none.

My son Josh called me one day to say;
I have a new girl friend I want you to meet and her name is Shay.

When and where did you meet I asked of him;
We met at school on the campus of Texas A&M.

Where is she from, I did remark?
From up in Dallas a place called Highland Park.

A city, girly girl I thought inside;
What does she know of his cowboy ways and can she even ride?

He knows of those red dirt roads and good country air;
She knows of shopping malls and the latest trends to wear.

How could they even see eye to eye;
They came from different worlds, hers was so much citified.

Then that night in San Antonio I got to meet this sweet girl;
I could see in an instant she was now his whole world.

Her beauty and grace were beyond compare;
And much to my surprise she didn't seem to have a city girl airs.

Time went by and they were wed;
She became that cowboys dream it could be said.

My son the cowboy and this city girl found a true love from the
start;
To each other they give their complete love from their heart.

Now down life's highway with my blessings they ride together;
With God beside them they will prevail against any weather.

As down the life's dusty trail you do travel;
Pay close attention as the mysteries of life at times, God does
unravel.

Sometime a chance meeting can really be so much more;
It may even be the opening of loves door.

Keep your eyes open wide as you travel through life;
Maybe down that road is your husband or wife.

Yes that cowboy and the city girl found true love it seems;
And now spend their days, fulfilling each other's dreams.

God Bless you Josh and Shay and May all your trails be happy
forever and a day.

~~~

*Train up a child in the way he should go: and when he is old, he
will not depart from it. Proverbs 22:6*

*An excellent wife who can find? She is far more precious than
jewels. Proverbs 31:10*

*Whoso finds a wife finds a good thing, and obtains favor of
the LORD. Proverbs 18:22*

*Love is patient and kind; love does not envy or boast; it is not
arrogant or rude. It does not insist on its own way; it is not
irritable or resentful; it does not rejoice at wrongdoing, but rejoices
with the truth. Love bears all things, believes all things, hopes all
things, and endures all things. Love never ends.
1 Corinthians 13:4-8*

*Delight thyself also in the LORD: and he shall give thee the desires
of thine heart. Psalm 37:4*

Michael Gasaway

I Am Thankful

I am thankful but not just on Thanksgiving Day;
I'm thankful for all the blessings that God does send my way.

Take some time and make yourself a list of 10 things;
Include all that you're thankful for, especially those that make your
heart sing.

We all have so much to be thankful for as we travel through life;
Sometimes it's helpful to make a list that you can review in times
of strife.

Carry this list with you in your wallet or purse;
Then read it when you're in those times that just make you want to
curse.

Give thanks for all the things you have, both large and small;
Keep adding to your list throughout the year as you feel the call.

Your list should grow and grow as the years pass on by;
One day you'll read it and realize how your blessings seemed to
have multiplied.

Happy Thanksgiving to all my family and friends;
May ya'll be blessed today and always and that your list never
ends.

~~~

Do not be anxious about anything, but in everything by prayer and supplication with thanksgiving let your requests be made known to God. Philippians 4:6

I will give to the Lord the thanks due to his righteousness, and I will sing praise to the name of the Lord, the Most High. Psalm 7:17

Oh give thanks to the Lord, for he is good, for his steadfast love endures forever! Psalm 107:1

Giving thanks always and for everything to God the Father in the name of our Lord Jesus Christ, Ephesians 5:20

A Psalm for giving thanks. Make a joyful noise to the Lord, all the earth! Serve the Lord with gladness! Come into his presence with singing! Know that the Lord, he is God! It is he who made us, and we are his; we are his people, and the sheep of his pasture. Enter his gates with thanksgiving, and his courts with praise! Give thanks to him; bless his name! For the Lord is good; his steadfast love endures forever, and his faithfulness to all generations.
Psalm 100:1-5

A Thankless Job

A thankless job they have and are hardly paid enough to get by;
But year after year they do their best and each day continuing to try.

Each year more is expected of them than it was just the year before;
The demands and expectations are raised but the pay is never any more.

They must wear many hats and play so many roles each day;
Letting their administrators know that it can't continue this way.

But it stays the same as year after year it goes with no change in sight;
Some countries revere these people and hold them on high for doing what's right.

Here in America however we have let their stature slowly slip further away;
Hardly are they respected and we wonder why everything is in such disarray.

Teachers are these special people that I write of in this rhyme;
Can't you remember back when student discipline was expected back in a better time.

So many things have changed in the educational system over the years;
Now students graduate and are not even ready for their future careers.

No reflection on teachers for they have done the best with what they've been given;
In spite of it all, on they go doing the finest they can, not really expecting any appreciation.

Tomorrow give you child's teacher a special thank you for everything they do;
As parents do your part and install in your child discipline, respect and a Godly set of values.

Don't sit idly by and not let your school board know how you feel;
Speak up and support your teachers with all the things each day
they have to deal.

~~~

*And whatsoever ye do, do it heartily, as to the Lord, and not unto
men; Knowing that of the Lord ye shall receive the reward of the
inheritance: for ye serve the Lord Christ.
Colossians 3:23-24*

*And let us not grow weary of doing good, for in due season we will
reap, if we do not give up. Galatians 6:9*

*Train up a child in the way he should go: and when he is old, he
will not depart from it. Proverbs 22:6*

*In everything set them an example by doing what is good. In your
teaching show integrity, seriousness and soundness of speech that
cannot be condemned, so that those who oppose you may be
ashamed because they have nothing bad to say about us.
Titus 2:7-8*

*I will instruct you and teach you in the way you should go; I will
counsel you with my eye upon you. Psalm 32:8*

*May my teaching drop as the rain, my speech distill as the dew,
like gentle rain upon the tender grass, and like showers upon the
herb. Deuteronomy 32:2*

*You call me Teacher........, and you are right, for so I am.
John 13:13*

Michael Gasaway

Listen to the Music

Listen to the music as the rhythm flows through your ears;
Some songs will bring a smile and some will bring a tear.

All will touch you in one way or the other it seems;
Music is a part of us all and for some it drives their dreams.

Can you imagine how boring life would be without music in its
various forms?
Why if you listen there is even music that God has placed inside
thunderstorms.

Falling drops of rain on a tin roof just seems to sing;
Or maybe it's listening to the birds on an early morning spring.

Music is all around us and a part of us just listens to be satisfied;
Songs can bring such joy in life and some remind you of the tears
you cried.

So really listen to the music and let it touch your heart and soul;
Can you feel it down deep as sometimes it seems to fill that hole.

If you play, sing or write the music that we all truly love;
Give thanks to God for the gift you possess that He gave you from
above.

Then go out each day and night and give it all you've got to give;
Remember your music is touching people so let it show them how
to live.

Tell a story in music and rhyme and touch another's heart as you
play;
Let your music reach out to the multitudes from 6th street to
Broadway.

~~~

126

I will sing of steadfast love and justice; to you, O LORD, I will make music. Psalm 101:1

Sing unto him, sing psalms unto him: talk ye of all his wondrous works. Psalm 105:2

My lips shall greatly rejoice when I sing unto thee; and my soul, which thou hast redeemed. Psalm 71:23

And he hath put a new song in my mouth, even praise unto our God: Psalm 40:3

I will sing unto the LORD, because he hath dealt bountifully with me. Psalm 13:6

I will sing a new song to you, O God; upon a ten-stringed harp I will play to you, Psalm 144:9

To the music of the flute and the harp, to the melody of the lyre. Psalm 92:3

And behold, you are to them like one who sings lustful songs with a beautiful voice and plays well on an instrument, for they hear what you say, Ezekiel 33:32

Michael Gasaway

Your Promised Land

Sometimes in life you will reach the end of your preverbal rope;
That's when you should turn to God and He will help you cope.

There are days in life when you have to give it all you've got;
Just hang on to life's rope and then tie a big ole knot.

Rest your weary body, mind and soul and then just climb on;
Consider life not as a sprint you run but as a lifelong marathon.

No one ever said that life would be easy traveling down the trail;
Not getting back in the saddle of life is the only time you really
ever fail.

Life is full of choices and it's up to you which one you choose;
You were given free will and it's up to you to decide, win or lose.

You've been there before and faced tougher times than this;
Remember when God reached down and pulled you from that dark
abyss.

So never give up on life and always give it one more day;
Then turn your face to God and from your knees really, really pray.

Don't ask God to make the road easy that you now travel along;
Rather to give you strength and to make you emotionally strong.

Then one day before you if you don't get weak, there they will
stand;
Your heart's desire, your dreams realized and your promised land.

~~~

Be careful for nothing; but in everything by prayer and supplication with thanksgiving let your requests be made known unto God. And the peace of God, which passes all understanding, shall keep your hearts and minds through Christ Jesus. Philippians 4:6-7

For I know the thoughts that I think toward you, saith the LORD, thoughts of peace, and not of evil, to give you an expected end. Jeremiah 29:11

No temptation has overtaken you that is not common to man. God is faithful, and he will not let you be tempted beyond your ability, but with the temptation he will also provide the way of escape, that you may be able to endure it. 1 Corinthians 10:13

Trust in the Lord with all thine heart; and lean not unto thine own understanding. In all thy ways acknowledge him, and he shall direct thy paths. Proverbs 3:5-6

And let us not grow weary of doing good, for in due season we will reap, if we do not give up. Galatians 6:9

Delight thyself also in the LORD: and he shall give thee the desires of thine heart. Psalm 37:4

Michael Gasaway

Priorities

Their love started out so fresh and pure as if from some romantic
dream;
Then slowly over time they drifted apart as things started to
unravel at the seams.

Neither really took notice of what was happening to them at the
time;
Both had their careers and kids and their priorities were no longer
aligned.

Communication was the first casualty as the years slowly slipped
by;
Mobile devices took the place of conversation except for a quick
peck and goodbye.

You see it everywhere you go now days, people holding phones
instead of each other;
They can tell you what's happening in China but not with one
another.

I think it's the moment and I'm sure many will agree that it's way
overdue;
It's time to put the phones away and have a loving conversation,
just you two.

It won't take long and a difference you will truly begin to see;
You'll stop taking each other for granted and remember back to
how it used to be.

That's just one step of many that you both must take along the
way;
Like holding hands and showing your love in both the deeds and
words you say.

Kiss passionately and often and dance in the rain every chance you
get on a rainy day;
Dance together and let the rain wash away the doubts and fears
you gathered along the way.

Love and desire will blossom again as it was just dormant and not
really gone at all;
You have no time to wait as you both must work at it so back
deeply in love you'll fall.

~~~

*Let no corrupting talk come out of your mouths, but only such as is
good for building up, as fits the occasion, that it may give grace to
those who hear. Ephesians 4:29*

*Let your speech be always with grace, seasoned with salt, that ye
may know how ye ought to answer every man. Colossians 4:6*

*I had much to write to you, but I would rather not write with pen
and ink. I hope to see you soon, and we will talk face to face.
3 John 1:13-14*

*And be ye kind one to another, tenderhearted, forgiving one
another, even as God for Christ's sake hath forgiven you.
Ephesians 4:32*

*Search me, O God, and know my heart: try me, and know my
thoughts: And see if there be any wicked way in me, and lead me
in the way everlasting. Psalm 139:23-24*

*Let him kiss me with the kisses of his mouth: for thy love is better
than wine. Song of Solomon 1:2*

Do everything in love. 1 Corinthians 16:14

Michael Gasaway

Not Red and Pink but Solid Gold

For some it's a holiday full of love and happiness;
Then for others it's just another day of past heartaches they'd
rather miss.

Would this day be different she wondered within her heart;
Could this be the year that she was given a fresh new start?

It had been so long since she had felt love in her heart, if at all;
So many years now, she had built the walls, so as not to fall.

She couldn't explain how he got through and touched her heart;
But here she was smiling and at the same time fearful of falling
apart.

Falling for this cowboy that had touched her with his words down
into her very soul;
Smiling she realized that this Valentine's Day was not red and pink,
but solid gold.

So keep your dreams and the true desires of your heart alive;
Then at last when you least expect it, you'll awaken to loves prize.

On that day you'll realize the journey down life's highway was
worth it all;
As He did lift you up and never really did let you fall.

Now on she goes with the love of her life, hand n' hand into a
future so bright;
With a smile as big as Texas, walking together with her new love
into a romantic Valentine's Day night.

~~~

Delight yourself in the LORD, and he will give you the desires of your heart. Psalm 37:4

Let all that you do be done in love. 1 Corinthians 16:14

Love is patient and kind; love does not envy or boast; it is not arrogant or rude. It does not insist on its own way; it is not irritable or resentful; it does not rejoice at wrongdoing, but rejoices with the truth. Love bears all things, believes all things, hopes all things, and endures all things. Love never ends.
1 Corinthians 13:4-8

And over all these virtues put on love, which binds them all together in perfect unity. Colossians 3:14

Anyone who does not love does not know God, because God is love. 1 John 4:8

A new commandment I give to you, that you love one another:" just as I have loved you, you also are to love one another. By this all people will know that you are my disciples, if you have love for one another." John 13:34-35

So now faith, hope, and love abide, these three; but the greatest of these is love. 1 Corinthians 13:13

Michael Gasaway

Special Fall Day

The dark clouds came rushing in across the parched dry Texas
plains;
As she surveyed the horizon, Lord knows she thought, we sure
could use some rain.

Having been a widow for some time now and everyone urged her
to give up and sell out;
That was not her way and maybe now the end was coming to this
long severe drought.

Ranching is no easy way of life to be sure especially in this day n'
time;
Being a woman alone made it sometimes harder even if she still
was in her prime.

She'd had a few suitors over the years but none could ever pass
her test;
In her mind it wasn't that difficult to constantly stand tall, do
what's right and always give your best.

Give your best in work but also to each other and to convey your
love;
Why men but especially cowboys couldn't understand she
questioned to God above.

Into town she went one fall day which for her was such a special
treat;
It wasn't often she got away from the ranch and never expected
this cowboy to meet.

He was ahead of her and held the door open, tipped his hat and
smiled;
Wow she thought as her heart skipped a beat feeling somewhat
beguiled.

She glanced his way a time or two and smiled as he sat across the
way drinking coffee alone;
After a bit he again smiled, tipped his hat as he walked out the
door and was gone.

Calling the waitress over for her check so that she could pay;

134

Smiling the waitress told her that the handsome cowboy paid and
said, "have a blessed day".

Along the street she walked but couldn't shake that special cowboy
off her mind;
Then around the corner he walked as their eyes locked on one
another each feeling this was divined.

The years have gone by and their tenth anniversary they will soon
celebrate together;
Side by side they have stood facing adversity and the harshest of
weather.

They both remember back when their paths crossed in that small
café;
Always thanking God above for bringing them together on that
special fall day.

~~~

Do everything in love.1 Corinthians 16:14

*And let us not grow weary of doing good, for in due season we will
reap, if we do not give up. Galatians 6:9*

*And we know that all things work together for good to them that
love God, to them who are the called according to his purpose.
Romans 8:28*

*And whatsoever ye do in word or deed, do all in the name of the
Lord Jesus, giving thanks to God and the Father by him.
Colossians 3:17*

*Rejoice evermore. Pray without ceasing. In everything give thanks:
for this is the will of God in Christ Jesus concerning you.
1 Thessalonians 5:16-18*

Michael Gasaway

Starting Over

Starting over is never easy and is filled with its own special pain;
But on you must go, through the tears you now cry like rain.

The memories will haunt you as they creep into your mind;
These too will fade away if you just give it some time.

Time heals all I've heard it said over the years;
I know its hard now to see a vivid future though your tears.

But better days will come if you just keep moving on;
A brighter potential you'll see one day with a brilliant new dawn.

It won't be easy but nothing worthwhile never is it seems;
Just keep riding into tomorrow in search of your hopes and
dreams.

There will be good days and yes some days will be bad;
Keep trusting in God and try not to be sad.

God will lead, guide and direct you if you just ask Him too;
Yes even the pain you now feel He will help you through.

So never give up and each day put a smile on your face;
A brighter future awaits you, one you'll see with Gods amazing
grace.

Then thank God for the new life and blessings you now see;
It's always up to us to just perceive and really believe.

~~~

Christ hath made us free, and be not entangled again with the yoke of bondage. Galatians 5:1

And God shall wipe away all tears from their eyes; and there shall be no more death, neither sorrow, nor crying, neither shall there be any more pain: for the former things are passed away. Revelation 21:4

For I reckon that the sufferings of this present time are not worthy to be compared with the glory which shall be revealed in us. Romans 8:18

Delight thyself also in the LORD: and he shall give thee the desires of thine heart. Psalm 37:4

The heart of man plans his way, but the LORD establishes his steps. Proverbs 16:9

And let us not grow weary of doing good, for in due season we will reap, if we do not give up. Galatians 6:9

But without faith it is impossible to please him: for he that cometh to God must believe that he is, and that he is a rewarder of them that diligently seek him. Hebrews 11:6

Welcome My Friend

The difference between your ears can be so different and vast;
From the inside or out between them there is such a great
contrast.

Distance between your ears on the outside is what you'll see;
But the space on the inside between your ears is what you'll
believe.

You see with your eyes or you can also see with your soul;
It's up to you and how you view the world, you have control.

Thus control the view of the world that you want to perceive;
In the end what your view will be, is also what you'll achieve.

Your perception of reality is what you alone get to choose;
In the end it could decide if you in fact get to win or lose.

We are all given the choice of free will in our life;
Sometimes it's our own actions that will take us into strife.

So when a choice you have to make along life's highway;
Pray to God making the right decision for your life and never be
afraid.

Keep in constant prayer and ask God to direct your steps each day;
He will always walk with you and He'll show you the right way.

Then He'll be there to pick you up and take you home in the end;
God will greet you with open arms and say "Welcome my Friend".

~~~

Stand fast therefore in the liberty wherewith Christ hath made us free, and be not entangled again with the yoke of bondage. Galatians 5:1

He shall not be afraid of evil tidings: his heart is fixed, trusting in the LORD. Psalm 112:7

Now faith is the substance of things hoped for, the evidence of things not seen. Hebrews 11:1

And all things, whatsoever ye shall ask in prayer, believing, ye shall receive. Matthew 21:22

Now the God of hope fill you with all joy and peace in believing, that ye may abound in hope, through the power of the Holy Ghost. Romans 15:13

A man's heart devises' his way: but the LORD directs his steps. Proverbs 16:9

For therefore we both labor and suffer reproach, because we trust in the living God, who is the Savior of all men, especially of those that believe. 1 Timothy 4:10

Michael Gasaway

A New Spring

The flowers are starting to bloom and the trees are turning green;
It's a new beginning for her, a new life not just a new spring.

He came into her life at a time when she was feeling so down;
Sinking deeper and deeper she was feeling she just might drown.

Pulling her up from the depths she had sunken from that dark
abyss so deep;
The words he had spoken gave her hope, awakening her from a
cavernous sleep.

Learning a real faith, hope and love she'd never known really
existed;
When she felt like giving up it was then her earthly angel just
persisted.

He pushed her on each day striving to bring out her best within;
Even on those days when all she wanted was to give up and give
in.

Time has moved on and she has achieved many of her heart's
desire;
Looking back it brings a smile to her face as she stares into the
bonfire.

Sometimes that cowboy crosses her mind as she remembers his
words in rhyme;
"Keep moving forward and always be looking for another dream to
find.

Sit tall in the saddle, with your heals down and head up high;
Move on each day and just enjoy this life we call the ride.

Keep your eyes on the horizon where the earth meets the sky;
It's your life to live so really live it as He will always be by your
side."

Now's she faces each day with a smile on her beautiful face;
She's putting her complete faith and trust in God and His loving
grace.

~~~

For behold, the winter is past; the rain is over and gone. The flowers appear on the earth, the time of singing has come, and the voice of the turtledove is heard in our land.
Song of Solomon 2:11-12

For I know the thoughts that I think toward you, saith the LORD, thoughts of peace, and not of evil, to give you an expected end.
Jeremiah 29:11

Now faith is the substance of things hoped for, the evidence of things not seen. Hebrews 11:1

Be not forgetful to entertain strangers: for thereby some have entertained angels unawares. Hebrews 13:2

Beloved, I pray that all may go well with you and that you may be in good health, as it goes well with your soul. 3 John 1:2

May he give you the desire of your heart and make all your plans succeed. Psalm 20:4

But I trusted in thee, O Lord: I said Thou are my God. My times are in thy hand: deliver me from the hand of mine enemies, and from them that persecute me. Psalm 31:14-15

And whatever you ask in prayer, you will receive, if you have faith. Matthew 21:22

Therefore I say unto you, what things so ever ye desire, when ye pray, believe that ye receive them, and ye shall have them.
Mark 11:24

Michael Gasaway

Back to Texas

He walked around the lake shore taking in the beauty of the
autumn leaves;
But they only made him homesick of the one place he truly longed
to be.

Back to Texas is where his heart was and where he wanted to go;
Going back in time he remembered walking as a child along the
river Frio.

He'd made up his mind now and soon he'd again be headed back
home;
Once back in Texas from her he didn't think he'd ever again roam.

His heart and spirit were now healed and it was time to head back;
The truck was ready and now all he had to do was pack.

Traveling west bound that Texas moon shinning so bright leading
the way;
With the rising of the morning sun he'd be back in Texas forever to
stay.

Sunrise was highlighting the sign as he saw it up ahead on the
road side;
His heart was beating faster as unconsciously faster as he also did
drive.

A big cowboy grin came across his face as he crossed that Texas
line;
This was where he belonged and knew that here he'd stay for all
time.

Into Buc-ees he pulled for gas and get some coffee for a brake;
Gone it seems now were all his troubles and worries including his
heartache.

It didn't take long for everything to come together and really fall
into place;
There she stood with midnight hair and bluebonnet eyes and filled
with a certain Texas grace.

Their hearts both touched even before their eyes met each other;
This was their destiny as in the following weeks they'd soon
discover.

The years have since gone by and their love has grown stronger
each day;
Daily they thank God for bringing them together along life's
highway.

~~~

*'The LORD your God is providing you a place of rest and will give
you this land.' Joshua 1:13*

*And we know that all things work together for good to them that
love God, to them who are the called according to his purpose.
Romans 8:28*

A happy heart makes the face cheerful, Proverbs 15:13

*From the rising of the sun unto the going down of the same
the LORD's name is to be praised. Psalm 113:3*

A joyful heart is good medicine, Proverbs 17:22

*Whether therefore ye eat, or drink, or whatsoever ye do, do all to
the glory of God. 1 Corinthians 10:31*

*And over all these virtues put on love, which binds them all
together in perfect unity. Colossians 3:14*

*Delight thyself also in the LORD: and he shall give thee the desires
of thine heart. Psalm 37:4*

Gentle Kiss

One day when you least expect it, true love will come knocking at
your door;
It will fill you with emotions and a love you've never felt before.

It may come softly, as a spring breeze caresses your face;
Or arrive as a shooting star that just seems to appear touching you
with a special grace.

Most often it catches you unaware and when you're not really
looking for love;
Then there it is straight to your heart, cupids arrow finds you from
above.

Both of your emotions will be rocked as cautiously forward into
love together you go;
Then you'll awake one day and realize that true love has touched
your soul.

A bright smile you'll wear that comes deep within your heart;
With this one special other you've found and from them you'll
never want to part.

Now hand n' hand you both go into tomorrow feeling love's bliss;
You'll count your blessings, when you feel upon your lips their
sweet kiss.

So never give up on life or that one true love your destined to find;
One day into your life they will ride when the stars become aligned.

Your eyes will be opened wide and your soul will be changed on
that blessed day;
A new life begins with your true love that you were destined to find
along life's highway.

~~~

And we know that for those who love God all things work together for good, for those who are called according to his purpose. Romans 8:28

Love is patient, love is kind. It does not envy, it does not boast, it is not proud. It does not dishonor others, it is not self-seeking, it is not easily angered, it keeps no record of wrongs. Love does not delight in evil but rejoices with the truth. It always protects, always trusts, always hopes, and always perseveres. Love never fails. 1 Corinthians 13:4-8

Let him kiss me with the kisses of his mouth: for thy love is better than wine. Song of Solomon 1:2

Whoever gives an honest answer kisses the lips. Proverbs 24:26

Steadfast love and faithfulness meet; righteousness and peace kiss each other. Psalm 85:10

Let us not become weary in doing good, for at the proper time we will reap a harvest if we do not give up. Galatians 6:9

Delight thyself also in the LORD: and he shall give thee the desires of thine heart. Psalm 37:4

Michael Gasaway

Faith and Courage to Win

He awoke with a start from another long night of bad dreams;
It's all he brought back from the war were memories and scars it
seems.

The outside wounds had healed and only the scars remained;
But inside the wounds ran deeper and he wondered if he'd ever be
the same.

Some days it was so hard to escape the pain and recollections he
carried within;
All he really wanted was to forget and go back in time and begin
again.

But there are no do over's and few second chances as we travel
through life's fate;
We have to play the cards we're dealt even if they are aces and
eights.

It's not what you're given in life but how you play the game that
really matters in the end;
Some hands you'll win and some you may lose but through it all
you must transcend.

You have to get beyond your haunting past and what you see as
the reality of today;
You're only passing through this valley of darkness so just asks
God to show you the way.

It won't be easy but the birth of new a life and beginnings never
are it seems;
Stepping out on faith and accepting a helping hand is the beginning
of chasing your dreams.

Your dreams aren't dead and neither are you unless you just give
up and give in;
But you're no quitter and you owe them the opportunity they'll
never have or the chances to win.

So do it for them and live the best life you can perceive coming
your way;
Let go and let God lead guide and direct your steps until your last
days.

146

Until then step out today and begin that new life that awaits you
with the faith and courage and a victor be;
Then one day God will welcome you home where you can reunite
with your brothers in arms for eternity.

~~~

*When the righteous cry for help, the Lord hears and delivers them
out of all their troubles. The Lord is near to the brokenhearted and
saves the crushed in spirit. Many are the afflictions of the
righteous, but the Lord delivers him out of them all. He keeps all
his bones; not one of them is broken. Psalm 34:17-20*

*For I will restore health unto thee, and I will heal thee of thy
wounds, saith the LORD; Jeremiah 30:17*

*Finally, be strong in the Lord and in the strength of his might. Put
on the whole armor of God that you may be able to stand against
the schemes of the devil. For we do not wrestle against flesh and
blood, but against the rulers, against the authorities, against the
cosmic powers over this present darkness, against the spiritual
forces of evil in the heavenly places. Therefore take up the whole
armor of God that you may be able to withstand in the evil day,
and having done all, to stand firm. Stand therefore, having
fastened on the belt of truth, and having put on the breastplate of
righteousness ... Ephesians 6:10-18*

*Yea, though I walk through the valley of the shadow of death, I will
fear no evil: for thou art with me; thy rod and thy staff they
comfort me. Psalm 23:4*

*And let us not grow weary of doing good, for in due season we will
reap, if we do not give up. Galatians 6:9*

*Verily, verily, I say unto you, He that hears my word, and
believeth on him that sent me, hath everlasting life, and shall not
come into condemnation; but is passed from death unto life.
John 5:24*

Michael Gasaway

Christmas

There has been many a Christmas I spent in far off distant lands;
I've even spent Christmas under the palm trees with my toes in the
sand.

Seen the snow fall from the sky, on Christmas Eve;
It was a time I was down, but it made me believe.

There have been Christmas's where I was lonely and sad;
Then there were a few where I felt so happy and glad.

It is a season that always takes us back in time;
The memories' always come flooding back into our mind.

You can't go back and change a Christmas from your past;
But you can start now by making new memories' that will last.

Start today where ever you may find yourself in life;
That means even if you're in the midst of life's storms and strife.

Just remember why we celebrate during this special season;
Your attitude will change when you really discover and live for the
true reason.

Celebrate the reason and make new memories that will light up
your face;
This is the time of the year for miracles and God's amazing grace.

Don't worry about how much you have to give;
What matters the most is how you will choose to live.

So live in such a way that through you, people will see God on
display;
Wish everyone you meet a Merry Christmas as you go about your
way.

Then when you look back on this time next year;
You'll remember that in your heart there was gladness and cheer.

Merry Christmas to all my family and friends far and near;
May God bless you and direct your steps in the coming year.

~~~

For unto us a child is born, unto us a son is given: and the government shall be upon his shoulder: and his name shall be called Wonderful, Counselor, The mighty God, The everlasting Father, The Prince of Peace. Isaiah 9:6

Saying, Where is he that is born King of the Jews? for we have seen his star in the east, and are come to worship him. Matthew 2:2

Now the birth of Jesus Christ took place in this way. When his mother Mary had been betrothed to Joseph, before they came together she was found to be with child from the Holy Spirit. And her husband Joseph, being a just man and unwilling to put her to shame, resolved to divorce her quietly. But as he considered these things, behold, an angel of the Lord appeared to him in a dream, saying, "Joseph, son of David, do not fear to take Mary as your wife, for that which is conceived in her is from the Holy Spirit. She will bear a son, and you shall call his name Jesus, for he will save his people from their sins." All this took place to fulfill what the Lord had spoken by the prophet: Matthew 1:18-25

And going into the house they saw the child with Mary his mother, and they fell down and worshiped him. Then, opening their treasures, they offered him gifts, gold and frankincense and myrrh. Matthew 2:11

For unto us a child is born, unto us a son is given: and the government shall be upon his shoulder: and his name shall be called Wonderful, Counselor, The mighty God, The everlasting Father, The Prince of Peace. Isaiah 9:6

Michael Gasaway

Choose Your Words Wisely

Waves of light from the early dawn came streaming through the
trees;
Rolling over the hill sides he could feel the hint of autumn on the
breeze.

Soon the ever changing of the seasons would bring briskness to
the mountain air;
Unlike in years past he now looked forward to this fall without a
care.

His journey down life's highway had taken him far and wide over
the years;
He reflected back in time mostly with fondness but yes even with
some tears.

The years seemed to be coming faster now though a little slower
he seemed to be;
Now he viewed each sunrise with the anticipation of hopes and
dreams and of all the possibilities.

Physically his strength may not have been the same as his youth
back in the day;
But spiritually and emotionally the stronger he had become with
each of life's challenges along the way.

Each morning now for years he greeted each day with a cup of hot
coffee and that same ole cowboy grin;
Remembering back as a young man when he was told, "Your days
will be a reflection of what you carry within."

That ole' cowboy had been full of old stories, yarns and good
advice it seems;
Funny how as we grow older looking back we realize how they
shaped our dreams.

Choose your words wisely and the advice you impart as you travel
through life;
You may never realize the impact your words may have had
helping another through good times and strife.

So always keep a smile on your face and let your expressions show
joy and love;

Give thanks to God each day for showing you the way in which to travel life's highway and dusty trails from above.

~~~

Do not be anxious about anything, but in everything by prayer and supplication with thanksgiving let your requests be made known to God. Philippians 4:6

Whatever you do, work at it with all your heart, as working for the Lord, not for human masters, Colossians 3:23

And be not conformed to this world: but be ye transformed by the renewing of your mind, that ye may prove what is that good, and acceptable, and perfect, will of God. Romans 12:2

Sanctify them through thy truth: thy word is truth. John 17:17

Listen to advice and accept instruction, that you may gain wisdom in the future. Proverbs 19:20

Let no corrupt communication proceed out of your mouth, but that which is good to the use of edifying, that it may minister grace unto the hearers. Ephesians 4:29

Rejoice in hope, be patient in tribulation, be constant in prayer. Romans 12:12

Delight thyself also in the LORD: and he shall give thee the desires of thine heart. Psalm 37:4

In everything give thanks: for this is the will of God in Christ Jesus concerning you. 1 Thessalonians 5:18

Michael Gasaway

God Bless America

We salute today the red, white and blue;
Our nation's colors, those that have always run true.

Our country was founded over 200 years ago today;
Let us take time to thank God, and for our country do pray.

Hard times she has faced and wars she has fought to stay free;
It is the price we willingly paid for our liberty.

Let us never forget the lessons our fore fathers tried to teach;
Success in this great country is always within our reach.

We became a nation of laws and doing what's right;
Sometimes we faltered and failed to see the light.

Today should be a day of reflection and praise to be given;
If not for the brave men then free we would not be livin'.

Our flag has flown over many lands and on every sea;
Let us never forget the price many paid to be free.

Many will go to different places to celebrate with fireworks in the
sky;
Take time to remember and reflect on why.

Celebrate and enjoy this day with a reverence pause;
For if we forget why, then we just may become a lost cause.

We came from many countries to become one nation of the brave;
Let us also remember this day the price that was paid.

It was to God that our fore fathers did pray and give thanks above;
If we forget, then we may cease to receive His divine love.

So take a moment during all your celebrating today and say a
prayer;
That once again we show God how much we really care.

Put your hands together and do pray with me;
That once again God will smile down on us favorably.

Enjoy your day and have lots of fun;
But never forget that without God we would never have begun.

May God Bless America this day and always with His love;
May He once again smile upon us and bless us from above.

~~~

If my people who are called by my name humble themselves, and pray and seek my face and turn from their wicked ways, then I will hear from heaven and will forgive their sin and heal their land.
2 Chronicles 7:14

"And if you faithfully obey the voice of the Lord your God, being careful to do all his commandments that I command you today, the Lord your God will set you high above all the nations of the earth. And all these blessings shall come upon you and overtake you, if you obey the voice of the Lord your God. Blessed shall you be in the city, and blessed shall you be in the field. Blessed shall be the fruit of your womb and the fruit of your ground and the fruit of your cattle, the increase of your herds and the young of your flock. Blessed shall be your basket and your kneading bowl. ...
Deuteronomy 28:1-68

"At that time shall arise Michael, the great prince who has charge of your people. And there shall be a time of trouble, such as never has been since there was a nation till that time. But at that time your people shall be delivered, everyone whose name shall be found written in the book. Daniel 12:1

And nations shall come to your light, and kings to the brightness of your rising. Isaiah 60:3

Blessed is the nation whose God is the Lord, the people whom he has chosen as his heritage! Psalm 33:12

Righteousness exalts a nation, Proverbs 14:34

Michael Gasaway

Sometimes God Just Says No

Yes, sometimes God just says no;
The reasons why we may never fully comprehend or know.

No, just because its time and His will, is the hardest when this He
does convey;
Whatever the reason, no is very difficult to accept so just go to him
and pray.

It may be to keep us safe from harm along the way;
Maybe it was to steer us from hurtful words someone may say.

You may not have been ready for that situation to be in your life;
Inside you were still dealing with your own adversity and strife.

Perhaps someone's choices and decisions caused God to speak;
Standing right with you during times you were weak.

Sometimes the no is "not right now my child, just wait";
He's giving you time for your choices to contemplate.

Your fear occasionally takes control and that's why He's saying no
this time;
In your heart you had let fear and pain control your mind.

Confusion will rock your world as round 'n round you go;
That's the time you really should turn to God and ask Him to show;

Ask God to truly show you the way that it should really be;
Turn it all over to Him and soon He will open your eyes so that you
will see.

He will lead guide and direct your steps down life's highway and
every dusty trail;
So always put your trust in Him to start with and you He will never
fail.

Then NO will never be a word you'll ever fear from God above;
As the path you are now following will be directed by His unfailing
love.

~~~

And we know that all things work together for good to them that love God, to them who are the called according to his purpose. Romans 8:28

This is the confidence we have in approaching God: that if we ask anything according to his will, he hears us. 1 John 5:14

For by grace are ye saved through faith; and that not of yourselves: it is the gift of God: Ephesians 2:8

Every good gift and every perfect gift is from above, and cometh down from the Father of lights, with whom is no variableness, neither shadow of turning. James 1:17

Better is the end of a thing than its beginning, and the patient in spirit is better than the proud in spirit. Ecclesiastes 7:8

Trust in the Lord with all thine heart; and lean not unto thine own understanding. In all thy ways acknowledge him, and he shall direct thy paths. Proverbs 3:5-6

For we walk by faith, not by sight 2 Corinthians 5:7

For therein is the righteousness of God revealed from faith to faith: as it is written, The just shall live by faith. Romans 1:17

God is a Spirit: and they that worship him must worship him in spirit and in truth. John 4:24

Now the God of hope fill you with all joy and peace in believing, that ye may abound in hope, through the power of the Holy Ghost. Romans 15:13

23462810R00089

Made in the USA
Columbia, SC
13 August 2018